Drilling for Wine

Drilling for Wine

Robin Yapp

faber and faber
LONDON · BOSTON

First published in 1988
by Faber and Faber Limited
3 Queen Square London WC1N 3AU

Phototypeset by Wilmaset Birkenhead Wirral
Printed in Great Britain by
Mackays of Chatham Kent
All rights reserved

British Library Cataloguing in Publication Data

Yapp, Robin
Drilling for wine.——(Wine series).
1. Wine and wine making——Great Britain
I. Title   II. Series
380.1'456632'00924   HD9381.5

ISBN 0–571–14760–7

For Judith

Contents

List of Illustrations

Photographs taken by Robin Yapp

Foreword

This is the second of my old friend Robin's books: the first, *Vineyards and Vignerons*, was written in collaboration with his wife, Judith, and illustrated and decorated by Charles Mozley, another old friend and just such another as Robin — as large as life, twice as natural and a considerable enhancer of it.

I suppose I should declare an interest, in that I am mentioned in that book and in this. Who am I to suspect tongue in cheek when in the first I am described as 'witty, wise and handsome'? Accurate reporting is good reporting, though I have to admit that in the second book it is blunted by the author's undue regard for an old friend's feelings: to call me 'shortish, stoutish' is too kind – the fact is that I am *very* short and noticeably stout (one is reminded of Jonathan Miller's 'not a Jew – only *Jewish*'.) No tongue in cheek, then, but perhaps sting in tail. In the first book it is claimed that, worsted in an argument about the use of Ribena in making Kir, I lost face and never retracted. Of course I did not retract but, as I pointed out in the blurb I wrote, I did send the author a grossly offensive postcard.

This time it is related that, years later, I forgot who it was (Robin, of course), who stood me a bottle of Cockburn 1908 for my sixty-fifth birthday, the author's making no allowance for senile amnesia – and my sixty-fifth birthday was a long time ago – and the fact (though it is later related) that I don't like port.

On the whole, though, the author is pretty decent about wine journalists in general and especially, and rightly, about Eddie Penning-Rowsell of the *Financial Times* – as scholarly about music as the great, late Raymond Postgate was about the classics, more so about wine, and like Raymond, a rock of integrity.

What a pity that Robin got on the wrong side – a side rarely in evidence – of Andrew Graham, wine correspondent of *The Times* for ten years in the 1960s and early 70s, after having soldiered throughout the war (affectionately caricatured by Rex Whistler, a fellow Welsh Guardsman and much the same civilized sort of person, then at our Paris embassy in the Duff Coopers' time, and one of the wittiest of writers as two at least of his books, *The Club* and *The Regiment*, bear witness, and especially his dazzling parody of regimental histories, *The Queen's Malabars*, among its battle honours 'Wilson's Bluff' and 'Bollinger 1928'.)

It is a tribute to them and to Robin that small wine-growing families in the Rhône and the Loire have become friends as close as any of his neighbours in Wiltshire and fellow-members of the Garrick, and his descriptions of the dinners he has eaten with them and his frankness in admitting to the evenings of repletion and of fuddle make happy reading.

So does the account of his early years, many of them spent in term-time at the dental school of the University of Leeds and in vacations as *commis* waiter at Tom Laughton's Royal Hotel, Scarborough, where he became adept enough to succeed (where his mischievous colleagues had elaborately planned for him to fail) in filleting and serving eight Dover sole at table from an almost unsupportable silver dish, and where he was still naïve enough to have been long in perceiving that the *sommelier* 'fancied me something rotten'.

Robin fancied wine more than he did the wine-waiter: it was here that he fell in love with the stuff, and until only a couple of years ago he contrived, being a man of inexhaustible energy and determination (not that he says as much himself), to combine the profession of dentistry with the calling of a wine-shipper – in the latter, at any rate, by trial and error. The same qualities have served to create out of the derelict Milk Factory (formerly a brewery) of Mere, Wiltshire, one of the prettiest small country houses I have ever seen to have been fashioned and furnished by a contemporary of taste.

Impossible to list here all Robin's well-informed enthusiasms, but tempting to mention, at any rate, that he not only enjoys good grub but can cook it; cares about and collects pictures; and has a monumental collection of records and compact discs of every kind of music, some played, some composed, by close friends. The point is that he is a most companionable and stimulating companion, whether over the dinner-table, at a picnic in France – as recorded here – and even when he is driving one thither, at a hundred miles an hour on the wrong side of the road, both hands off the wheel as he gesticulates his enjoyment.

That is what the book is about – Robin is an enjoyer, and all his enjoyments are genuine. There is not a single high-falutin word here about wine, not a phrase that does not ring true. And that is why the book itself is an enjoyment – read on.

Albany, London, 1987   CYRIL RAY

Waiting for Wine

I was originally a dentist, the profession from which I retired just two years ago – after nearly a quarter of a century's practice in a small rural town in North Dorset. For eighteen years (sixteen of them concurrent with the dentistry) my other, very different, occupation has been that of a shipper of esoteric wines from the Rhône and Loire valleys of France. No prize will be awarded for guessing which has been the more amusing trade. Quite obviously, wine is a far more exotic and romantic commodity than aching teeth – although dentistry has its own work satisfactions, particularly in a small community – and I very much regretted it when a choice had finally to be made (although my patients may well have heaved a sigh of relief).

Like so many other happy wine-bibbers, I am a first-generation wine enthusiast. My parents never touched the stuff – indeed, I suspect that they hardly knew what it was. The only bottles that ever came into the parental home containing anything vaguely relating to wine were around Christmas, holding dubious dark brown liquids from far-flung parts of the Commonwealth: Empire so-called sherry, Australian port and other beverages of that ilk. No doubt it was a patriotic gesture on my father's part – but not really conducive to firing anyone with enthusiasm for the product of the grape (not that I can ever remember being given an opportunity to sample those sticky drinks). Otherwise, the standard tipple consisted of various forms of spirits, with an occasional beer to chase them down.

So, for me, wine was a completely unknown factor; goodness knows when I would have got around to making its acquaintance, if it had not been for some pre-dental school stints among the lowest echelons of the catering trade.

There is no doubt that what I learned at university has been useful through adult life; certainly, that training allowed me to qualify, and to begin to make my way. However, working as a waiter in two North Yorkshire seaside hotels taught me far, far more than could *any* formal education about the vagaries of human nature, the value and honour to be found in giving good service, but, best of all, of the existence of life-enhancing wine!

Raven Hall Hotel, at Ravenscar in North Yorkshire, stands high on the towering cliffs that form the southern spur of justly celebrated Robin Hood's Bay. Looking across the magnificent amphitheatre of rough moorland, with a wide panorama of ever-changing seascape, the hotel's setting and views are breathtakingly beautiful. Patently an ultra-fashionable and, no doubt, expensive summer venue for well-heeled West Riding industrialists and their families throughout the 1930s, Raven Hall had become a touch run down by the mid-1950s when I started the first of two summer seasons spent working there as a waiter – although the swimming pool, golf course and location ensured its continued popularity.

The restaurant was run by a quaint couple who had originally arrived at the hotel in its heyday as *commis* waiters at the age of sixteen – then my own age. Now distinctly past any normal retirement age, John, the *maître d'hôtel*, and his long-term 'best friend', Peter, still showed the desire to cling (in ever-increasing desperation) to faint vestiges of part of the establishment's former glory – full traditional 'silver service'; neither was able to persuade the motley crew of non-English-comprehending continentals who formed the greater part of the complement of waiters, or a residual handful of surly Yorkshire-men, to share their dedication to old-fashioned virtues, such as lugging around large piles of heavy Victorian silverware.

The advent of a naïve and fairly willing postulant brought what might almost have passed for a smile to the normally immobile features of the taciturn *maître d'hôtel*.

As for the diminutive Peter, he joyously relished the unlooked-for opportunity to communicate to another the near-obsolete skills of the fancy ways of service of a former age. My Italian, Spanish and Yorkshire colleagues were vastly amused by my indoctrination, but wanted no part of it; with unwavering inflexibility, they maintained their rigid determination not to participate in such high-flown nonsense. The only person who truly resented the incursion of an enthusiastic newcomer so innocently prepared to indulge the old men in their anachronistic nostalgia was probably the washer-up who, professionally, occupied a rabbit-hutch of a room that would have shocked a Dickens or a Mayhew by its sheer squalor, and by the appalling heat and humidity in which the poor fellow was expected to ply his horrid trade; his was the task of searching out, resurrecting and rendering immaculate a whole battery of long-disused large chafing dishes and massive metal chargers, encrusted with the grease and grime of many years, all unearthed from unlikely nooks and crannies in the complex service quarters.

The serving dishes once again sparkling (or mildly reflective, anyway), my waiting education was taken in hand. Surprisingly, the whole rigmarole proved to be great fun, at least at first; as the months passed there were moments when the niceties became tedious, not to say downright arduous, to the dutiful student waiter. A routine that struck me as being particularly flashy, a chance to show off newly acquired adeptness, was that of painstakingly dissecting a Dover sole into succulent, boneless fillets at table – the trick being to deliver each fillet to the plate in one perfect piece. My considerable self-satisfaction at my new-found skill at this particular little cabaret number – always well received by the audience – eventually led to the sort of 'come-uppance' that such hubris deserves and, in my case, usually attracts . . . as will be seen later.

The two lengthy stints at Ravenscar were enormously and valuably instructive: it is certain that total immersion in such a volatile and combative community, toiling in sometimes difficult circumstances, teaches more about the necessity and importance of quick adaptation to life with other hard-pressed individuals, and about the strains of responding positively and pleasantly to the whims, vagaries and occasional downright bloody-mindedness of the paying customers than anything that can be gained from places of formal learning. Although Raven Hall taught me many useful lessons, I learned nothing about wine – other than the fact of its existence. However, my unusual apprenticeship proved to be the key to what came after.

The Royal Hotel, poised in Regency splendour on Scarborough's St Nicholas Cliff, is the main thread in the tangled skein of events that ultimately pushed me into the world of wine. That august institution was owned at the time by Tom Laughton, brother of film actor Charles and scion of a well-known family of Scarborough hoteliers. During my second summer at Ravenscar, rare-enough days off were sometimes spent in Scarborough, twenty miles to the south. Passing the elegant stuccoed front of the Royal, one could see, through the main door, the imposing hotel hallway with its full quota of fine paintings from the famous Laughton collection, vast flower arrangements and the beautiful Regency double staircase. It all looked excessively appealing, as did the crisp formality of starched white napery on the handsomely furnished tables in the restaurant window. I conceived a strong wish to see what lay beyond these tantalizing glimpses, rapidly supplanted by a keen but irrational desire to work amidst such grandeur, to become part of the organizational fabric of what was patently a bastion of old-time excellence – the sort of pleasure palace that Raven Hall was said to have been twenty-five years earlier.

Quite how I succeeded in persuading the formidable Mr Laughton to deign to grant me even an interview I cannot now recall; many laboriously composed and painstakingly penned letters diffidently but persistently offered the (doubtful) benefit of my humble services and craved consideration for employment at the Royal during the following summer. Cheek *and* attrition finally paid off, when an appointment was conceded, to coincide with my next day off: the encounter was an unforgettable, terrifying experience. I am quite sure that Mr Laughton was as generous and as genial a person as one might hope to meet – on anything like *normal* terms, that is, with something approaching equality; as a nervous, inarticulate and under-qualified prospective employee, the odds were wildly stacked against me. I cannot say that further acquaintance lessened his ability to intimidate or to awe me; I simply took best care to present a profile so low as to create near-invisibility whenever the boss loomed into sight.

I got the job, but only after he extorted guarantees that were very nearly to wreck my embryonic university career. The oh-so-casually (but so very carefully *and* intentionally) dropped allusions to my knowledge of, not to say positively amazing deftness at, 'silver service' seemed to carry the day when the interviewer expressed his deep concern at the impropriety and inherent danger of taking, by his standards, a rank amateur on to the hotel staff. The enforced commitment was a promise not only to work right through the succeeding holiday season, but also during the conference periods either side of the summer season proper – periods of enormous

commercial importance to big hotels in larger resorts, but dangerously inconvenient to someone about to commence a five-year course
in dentistry. In the event, the agreed timetable was fulfilled in
Scarborough, but to the detriment of what was expected at dental
school, where expulsion on grounds of non-attendance was threaten-
ingly close on more than one occasion.

Transition to life and employment in a prestigious hotel was just as
problematic and painful as might have been imagined, but the place
itself (front-of-house, of course, not the rear quarters, which were as
grim as any institution where nothing has been changed or improved
for generations) was as enchanting as I had anticipated: not that
kitchen or waiting staff got more than an occasional glimpse of such
delights. The work was stimulating; the restaurant appeared to my
untutored eyes to be the epitome of high style and elegance; the
required standard of service awesomely professional – though a
present-day three-Michelin-rosetted hotelier might well be amused
to see what then passed for *haute cuisine*. And there was, of course, the
'silver service', my professed competence at which had been the
passport to my presence upon the premises. I do not think that my
efforts in that direction were so *very* much less able than I had
claimed, or *that* much worse than those of my fellow waiters – a
brigade of well-trained, long-term professionals – but I obviously
took myself far too priggishly seriously, to their slightly irritated
amusement.

Saturday night dinner is always fraught in a grand resort hotel;
absolutely everyone (tired, hungry and tetchy after the day's journey)
wants to be fed at the earliest opportunity and they pour into the
dining room at 7.30 p.m. Apart from sheer need, they also want to
check out the standard of the food. Subsequently there is a division
into the greedy and the thirsty – the thirstiest being prised from the
cocktail bar with great difficulty at the very last minute; customers
arrive in reasonably orderly dribs and drabs over the two-hour
dinner period, so that the meal becomes a relatively relaxed and
civilized affair. Saturday nights were notorious hell, barely support-
able strains being inflicted on waiters and on kitchen – where bedlam
reigned and service came to a virtual standstill, while the football
crowd of guests bayed ever more desperately for food.

On an early exposure to this unmitigated torture I had the

outrageous bad luck to entertain a family of eight, all of whom demanded Dover sole. Unfortunately my enjoyment of (well, to be frank, my lamentable self-satisfaction with) the Dover sole dissection routine had been noted by my colleagues, all long-term Royal employees who liked or cordially detested one another to whatever degree, but at least knew intimately each other's little ways, and had long ago learned to cope with various deficiencies or idiosyncrasies. My irruption into their ranks gave them, for once, a rare communal bond – for a time, at least: for the moment, their interest and energies were united in conceiving modest and minor ways in which to discomfort a youngster so wet behind the ears. One of them took time out from the stifling heat of the queue of frustrated waiters at the hotplate (all urgently attempting to inveigle long-ordered dishes from the reluctant hands of an equally distraught team of perspiring chefs, *sous-chefs* and *commis* chefs) to pay a furtive visit to the domain of the washer-up, a lugubrious fellow only a little less scandalously housed than his counterpart at Ravenscar. That the novelty of the quickly whispered suggestion appealed to him I can well imagine; absolutely *anything* to break the monotony of his thankless existence must have been most welcome. My first awareness of the conspiracy was when I was handed my shoal of long-awaited soles. The wretched fish were presented to me over the hotplate by a beaming head chef (never before seen to smile) on an amazing silver platter of staggeringly enormous size and weight – so huge that I could barely carry it, so vast that eight generous Dover soles could lie in glory *without touching one another.*

Realizing how much my self-centred attitude had merited this jest, I staggered (with difficulty; the salver would only *just* pass, horizontally, through the service door) into the brightly lit area of the restaurant, passed through the ranks of impatient would-be diners, towards my 'station' of five tables. Bright pink with embarrassment, all too aware that I would never live down the catastrophe, mentally composing my letter of resignation, I miserably started to perform the task that hitherto had been a minor joy.

Peter must have taught me well; after what seemed an hour, the family of eight had, on their now cold plates, fairly presentable portions of lukewarm fish. Only at this point did I raise my humiliated head, ready to stammer out ineffectual apologies, as best I might, to my other furiously waiting clients for the extra, now unacceptable delay. To my astonishment I beheld pleasantly smiling faces on every side, where last had been morose, complaining people. In some curious, inexplicable way my great distress and the unreasonableness of my Herculean chore had communicated itself to the bystanders and had gained their sympathy: the whole ghastly episode had become a sort of stage performance. My memory of the horrid occasion suggests (probably erroneously) that there might even have been a discreet flutter of applause as I carried away the bones and massive dish. Certainly that particular crowd of guests were remarkably civil and good-humoured for the duration of their holiday – *and* tipped quite well when they departed. How anyone even knew of the existence of the monster serving dish that had been lying hidden in a dim recess of the plate room for decades past was never revealed; how the washer-up succeeded in cleaning it in time is also a mystery. After that evening I never saw the beastly thing again. The incident might perhaps be equated with an apprentice test, a celebration to mark the successful termination of seven years' hard training by inflicting unspeakable indignities upon the unlucky lad. I instantly became more amenable to advice, finding it to be well intended and often helpful; the reaction of my work fellows was a discernible softening of attitude; life immediately became altogether more tolerable.

In my eyes, the Royal Hotel was as magnificent an establishment as I had imagined. Theoretically the public rooms were strictly out of bounds, but an infrequent errand would take me now and then through the fabulously elegant hall, with its fine railed galleries, imposing Corinthian pillars, glittering chandeliers, handsome serpentine double staircase, splendid furniture, dense masses of flowers and, above all, lovely paintings. Tom Laughton was renowned for his fine and valuable art collection, most of which he had astutely purchased at knock-down prices, sensing the significance that lay beneath thick accretions of ancestral grime, when professional dealers eschewed them with disdain. A permanent handyman was employed to look after the general fabric of the hotel, punctiliously maintaining the condition of the décor, inside and out, making emergency repairs to recalcitrant plumbing; in fact, turning his hand to any and everything that was required to keep an elaborate organization in working trim. Joe's paint loft workshop afforded me an occasional oasis, where it was possible to snatch a few minutes' calm in the course of hectic daily routine. Always ready for a chat, with a lifetime's experience and knowledge of hotel and owner at his disposition, he was an entertaining source of historical anecdote and good plain gossip. One day I was mildly surprised to see an elaborately gilt-framed picture resting on a makeshift easel, but distinctly alarmed to see the old chap dabbing at its dirt-encrusted surface with a pledget of cotton wool that he constantly remoistened in a jar of solvent. A portrait of a languidly disdainful young man in eighteenth-century rig was dimly discernible beneath deposits of smoke. Where Joe gently applied and rubbed his magic solution patches of bright colour began to emerge; it was engrossing to watch the slow, painstaking operation, and to see the haughty features of the youth take form after a century or more of anonymity. When I remarked in awe that such a fine painting might almost pass for a Gainsborough, my handyman friend applied his wodge of cotton wool to the lower right-hand corner of the canvas; casually, not bothering to remove his extinguished pipe from between clenched teeth, he grunted an affirmative. I was later told that I had witnessed the restoration to light of Richard Darley, painted by Thomas Gainsborough in 1783. Some years earlier our mutual employer had thought to develop the skills of this trusted worker, and had organized for him a spell of intensive training in the restoration and cleaning of paintings with a well-known London art dealer. The oils must have made an interesting change from Sandtex and emulsion.

Once, in what must have been an exceptionally magnanimous mood, an unusually benign Mr Laughton showed me his collection (I rather think that I must have asked for the treat). It was as fascinating a gallery tour as I have ever made; there, in profusion, were the works of names with which to conjure; Stubbs, Constable, Van Dyck, a cluster of Courbets. I saw my very first Richard Dadd – his now celebrated *Oberon and Titania* – recall a vast crowd-filled Frith, and rather guiltily and discreetly admired the charms of a huge *Judgement of Paris* by William Etty – a large acreage of canvas considerably enlivened by the generous curves and dimples of three robust, immodest maidens. I failed to realize the significance of the more contemporary works, and would love to have the chance to see them all again – my taste is considerably more catholic now than in my youth. Perhaps one reason for my lack of appreciation of the Matthew Smiths, the Sutherland, the Edward Bawdens, and others, had something to do with what I am still sure was a most regrettable obsession on the part of the collector. At some stage in the early 1950s Laughton had fallen under the spell of a Polish painter called Zdzislaw Ruszkowski. Laughton's unfortunate fanaticism had garnered many of the man's works: sixty or more large canvases, when I was working there. The restaurant bore the brunt of what was surely the most important and extensive collection of Ruszkowskis in the world; I saw them three times daily. Happily a self-selective amnesia has served to protect me from bad memories; I have vague recollections of uncomfortable angularity and monochrome monotony which may well be absolutely unfair. At the time I found the dozen or so products of the Pole's genius adorning my place of work stiflingly overpowering, repellent and absolutely hideous. Perhaps I would view them differently upon fresh encounter, but I would just as soon not risk the experiment; to my relief a dealer friend assures me that Ruszkowski remains eminently unsought after. Just as well for old Zdzislaw that Tom Laughton had such a passion for his product – he would probably have otherwise gone cold and hungry.

Inevitably I learned a great deal about a staggering variety of subjects in such a lively, hectic place. The most momentous discovery was that of wine – hitherto a completely unknown quantity, an arcane mystery. The Royal boasted an excellent cellar, though I never saw its subterrestrial location; acceptance of an invitation to view its vaulted spaces and bottle-filled bins would have been most imprudent, as may become apparent in later episodes. Fortunately for me, I purloined a copy of the wine list, a piece of printed ephemera that has become one of the most valued, redolently nostalgic items in my wine library. A charming, lively line drawing of a seaside pavilion (by Edward Bawden, I rather think) adorns the cover, the gazebo's canopy being surmounted by a cheeky, bottle-swigging cherub.

'Bordeaux (white)' offers Château Climens 1947 for 35s, with Yquem 1944 costing only an additional ten shillings. '(Red)' has a modest Château Leoville-las-Cases 1953 for 25s, Poyferré 1949 at 30s, Château Petrus 1953, Lynch Bages 1945 and Lafites 1948 and 1947 at 40s, 50s and 55s respectively; then, Oh ye Gods, the dizzy heights are reached with the 1934 vintages of Haut Brion and Mouton Rothschild for the neatly rounded sum of 60s – all this in 1959! An unattributed Châteauneuf-du-Pape gets turfed into the 'Burgundy (red)' section – absolutely typical of the crude usage accorded Rhône wines in those far-off times: Hermitage and Côte Rôtie do not figure in the line-up anywhere. With an again unpedigreed Nuits Saint Georges (no vintage shown) priced at 25s, I think that I would, if given the choice, have chosen to splurge my entire week's wage on one of the enticing Domaine de la Romanée Conti numbers that close the subdivision – either La Tache or Richebourg, both 1933, at 80s a time. The 'Various' bracket embraces a Spanish white (Alella), a Chianti, Egri Bikavér (a Hungarian red), a dry Tokay Szamrodini and Paarl South African hock – all at prices between 13s 6d and 15s. Uneasy doubts are raised by the realization that the hotel's acclaimed food might be washed down with various sparkling wines, the choice lying between effervescent versions of red burgundy, Moselle, Liebfraumilch and muscatel. With these dubious delights costing between 32s 6d and 35s, one can only hope that the paying customers had enough sense of self-preservation to stick to *vrai* champagne – in which the list is strong, starting with Pol Roger 'White Foil' at 42s. Krug Private Cuveé 1949 cost 60s: a wonderful wine, worth every penny, drinking marvellously well in 1959, as I can aver; it was the first champagne that ever passed my lips and was, that summer, pretty well the first drop I had tasted of *any* wine.

The contrast between the cosseted ease and elegant surroundings of the hotel's guests and the antediluvian horror of conditions behind the swinging service doors was scarcely imaginable; the gap between the two societies was unbridgeable and immense. The labyrinthine corridors and squalid service rooms of the hotel's hinterland cannot possibly have been as grim as my present recollection – *nothing* could have been as bad as that! Certainly, they were uncomfortably gloomy; the whole maze-like layout might have been designed by a malevolent architect to create maximum discomfort and inconvenience for its unfortunate denizens. If so, he succeeded admirably. Thank goodness that daily exposure to a twilight nightmare that would have had the Piranesi of the *Carceri d'invenzione* reaching enthusiastically for his drawing pad quickly began to seem quite normal; familiarity worked its anodyne effect. The one aspect of life on the seamy side of the green baize that always remained monstrously unacceptable was the staff food. It must have taken time (and not inconsiderable expertise) to forage for poor enough raw material which was then transmuted by sadistic specialists into unattractive and unappetizing gobbets of unthinkable origin swimming in watery, cabbage-impregnated, greasy broth. To my mind, these probably well-intended offerings were totally inedible . . . so I took to petty larceny.

One of the great truths of the catering industry is that no matter what, or however stringent, forms of control a zealous and anxious management may institute in an attempt to preserve their property, no waiter worthy of the epithet, no true member of that noble calling, has ever had to forgo any tasty morsel on the day's menu that happened to take his fancy. It is incredible how rapidly an education in self-help can be accomplished. So very speedily acquired is the art of making even the most substantial cut of meat vanish in a blink (leaving not the merest trace) that it must be by some process of professional osmosis. The first week of my career in Scarborough was barely halfway through before I had devised a scheme that would baffle the hard-pressed clerk whose permanent post, a desk on the kitchen side of the door between kitchen and restaurant, had been expressly established to arrest any nefarious change of ownership of the hotel's food. The poor chap ended up being the victim of his own elaborately contrived system of surveillance and check; ultimately there was too much paperwork. Basically the idea was that, once the seated guests had been persuaded to order, the waiter would make out an official docket carrying several carbon copies – a form of receipt which had to be exchanged with all concerned, the kitchen crew, eagle-eyed clerk, and so on. In due course the requested dish would be reluctantly discharged by the cooks, its transfer made official by initialling the ticket; the same irritating performance at the exit desk then permitted passage to the waiting diners. At busy times, when pieces of paper were being wildly brandished by one and all (rather like the flurry around on-course bookmakers at a provincial race meeting when the favourite has just romped home), it was simplicity itself to fudge the paperwork and gull the guileless clerk.

It had come to my notice that salmon was a pleasing victual, particularly so when freshly grilled; the notion of verifying this generally held assertion began to shape itself in my mind. The places where titbits can be cached are quite extraordinary; the dumb-waiter (very like the sort of counting house desk at which a clerk stood to wield his quill) that was the focal point of every waiter's 'station' could itself conceal an astonishing number of relatively bulky objects. Much later, when the room had been vacated and the lights all dimmed, I crept back to secure my prize and to savour its delights, beneath the disapproving glare of Ruszkowski's contorted models. To my astonishment an elegant bottle adorned my serving place, holding most of its precious contents; thus my first delighted experience of (by now cold) salmon was richly and unforgettably enhanced by, and joyously swilled down with, a highly appreciated excess of Krug Private Cuvée 1949. Magic might really make extraordinary events occur; fairies might truly roam the night-time world.

Aphrodisiacal Aperitifs

The head *sommelier* (referred to merely as head wine waiter in those simpler days) was a man of no little distinction, of great aplomb; indeed he was *majestic*. A tall, well-built fellow (though with an incipient tendency towards *embonpoint*), Michael was an Irishman, and had a knowing charm for those whom he chose to acknowledge. The obligatory full-fig evening 'tails' sat well upon his ample shoulders; the whole ensemble presented an intimidating spectacle to an impressionable youth. Even his own team of four subordinate wine waiters were fairly terrified on days when displeasure sat on his lordly brow. This symbol of authority proved to have been the mysterious donor of my vinous treat; he it was who was responsible for my baptism with wine. A smart party celebrating something or other in one of the private dining rooms failed to observe the subtle abstraction of one of their bottles of Krug, which was later to materialize upon my improvised dining table. The realization that I had been favoured by a slight inclination of the head from time to time, a slight crinkling of the lip that might just have been a smile, began to establish itself, and I guessed the source of my welcome beverage. That the high priest of wine must, after all, like me became increasingly manifest; what I stupidly failed to realize was that these charming gestures of goodwill signified a distinctly aberrant passion; the head wine waiter fancied me something rotten.

Strategies had soon to be adopted which permitted me to accept part-filled bottles of frequently excellent wine, the equivalent of pretty posies or bouquets, from my unlikely admirer with as much charm and apparent grace as I could counterfeit, all the while courteously declining urgent invitations to further our burgeoning acquaintance during off-duty hours. Lacking any conception that there were any such things as liaisons between men, I must have been preserved from a frightful fate by some residual wit and a strongly innate, though completely uncomprehending, sense of self-preservation. I spent the next few weeks dodging danger and compromise with (now I think about it) all the agility of a ballet dancer, all the while becoming more besotted with, and increasingly appreciative of, the qualities and virtues of good wine.

Only once did my ridiculous flirting with matters beyond my ken put me at more specific risk, but the incident opened my eyes very wide indeed. I shared a garret of a semi-dormitory under the roof of the hotel with a couple of *commis* chefs and a junior understudy washer-up, a ruffian from the Gorbals whose profanity-laced descriptions of past exploits (in the main part sexual and astonishingly lurid) were horrifying, but utterly fascinating. The lads from the kitchen were not much better, but the Scotsman held a wide lead in acquaintanceship with all things vile and evil. Jock (inevitably his name) was *hors concours* villain in our little society, and would probably have beaten all-comers drawn from the entire hotel community of Scarborough, if not the world. These interesting new chums got wind of my predicament and of course understood the situation completely, in a way that I did not; not that they thought to enlighten me – the opportunity for amusement was far too great.

On one of our late evening jaunts around the hostelries with which mid-town Scarborough abounds, one of my companions engineered our steps towards the Equestrian, a pub adjacent to the Playhouse stage door that I had never previously had occasion to explore. There in the bar parlour, ensconced in an appropriately throne-like chair, was my would-be friend, Michael, happily lording it over a sycophantic gaggle of thespian friends, and looking scarcely less impressive in roll-neck cashmere pullover and chunky gold necklace than in his workaday 'penguin' suit. We were summoned to join his court by a majestic flourish of an enormous cut glass goblet brimming with gin and tonic; libations were procured for us at his behest; a pint of Cameron's Strongarm bitter for each of my quartet (now and then it was customary to bolster that brew's already legendary potency by adding a barley wine to the contents of the glass).

A considerable time elapsed (it seemed to be a virtual licensing law that Scarborough pubs should never be closed to regular patrons, no matter what the hour) before Michael announced that his dear friend Patrick, compère and main star of a rather *outré* floor show that nightly enlivened the atmosphere of a neighbouring hotel, was urgently expecting us all, 'but *all* of us, darling', to attend a little soirée at his apartment. My attempts to demur and to organize a retreat to the safety of the hotel were completely undermined by my treacherous so-called friends, who were hell-bent on having some fun at my expense, if at all possible.

We weaved our way to Patrick's party where the ambience fitted my notion of an ambitious *fin-de-siècle* brothel fallen on hard times – red-shaded lamps, brocade cushions, a multitude of ornaments, sticky wine proffered in yet more cut glass, sultry music on the gramophone and a space cleared for slow-motion dancing. My intense sense of distress at being part of these peculiar festivities was intuitively and unerringly correct, as was hideously confirmed when the bearer of bottles, Michael, suggested that we dance – together! Finally my polite, increasingly strained but adamant refusal was accepted with exceedingly poor grace, but my resolution had suffered such an assault that I idiotically allowed myself to be dragged on to the dance floor by our host's girlfriend. A strapping but ill-favoured girl in a *diamanté*-encrusted black velvet gown, with raven tresses brushing her naked shoulders, the temptress slowly wheeled me round the floor to the strains of some cloying ballad of an earlier time. It crossed my mind as being distinctly bizarre that she should be sporting such a well-defined 'six o'clock shadow' upon her jutting jaw. Another anatomical oddity began to make itself apparent as this amazon clutched me ever more tightly to her chest; with sickening embarrassment it dawned upon me that our closeness had aroused my partner in a most unaccountable fashion. I tore myself from the strong embrace and fled the scene precipitately, literally pursued by Michael and several of his circle. Whether their wish was to apologize and to explain, I shall never know; an astonishing turn of speed put them out of sight in seconds.

My room mates returned a long time afterwards, still in an inebriated state of uncontrollable merriment at my near escape. From that time on I bought my own wine, rough Mâcon *rouge*, or an excruciatingly acidic Algerian *cru*, when not taking refuge in a judicious blend of Strongarm bitter and barley wine. The process of growing up had suffered an alarming burst of acceleration, but I was irretrievably hooked on good wine.

The great conundrum in those far-off, otherwise halcyon, Scarborough days was how on earth to divest oneself of one's innocence –

well, not to put too fine a point on matters, one's virginity (in the heterosexual sense, I hasten to add; the other way would have been all too easy, as we have seen). The apparently insuperable difficulty was that all the girls, right down to the last unemancipated young woman among them, were hanging on to theirs like grim death. Only a few years later – but too late in the day for us, alas – the next generation was at it hammer and tongs all day and all night, if the popular press might be believed. Nowadays it begins to seem as if it soon will be deemed imprudent to exchange the lightest, friendliest kiss without the protection of a polythene bag over everybody's head.

A black dustbin liner might well have made the young lady to whom I laid siege in the summer of 1959 distinctly more appealing; the object of my admittedly lustful ambitions, the proposed target for a first *real* skirmish of an amatory nature, boasted pallid features dusted with an unfortunate crop of acne – even her mother could hardly have proclaimed her a raving beauty. Nevertheless, Ethel enjoyed the reputation of being generous-natured and reasonably kind-hearted; she was also known to like a drink.

The fashionable aperitif that season was sherry, and highest in the popularity charts of high society was Tio Pepe – then, as now, an ultra-dry fino of considerable finesse. Wishing to enhance what I already fondly imagined to be an image of extraordinary sophistication, I procured a bottle of Tio Pepe as an accessory to my plan and proposed an evening stroll through one of the pleasant parks that contribute to the attractiveness of Scarborough as a resort. In due course, and at the appointed time, I awaited Ethel outside her place of employment: the public library. Upon her eventual arrival, I persuaded my friend to link arms with me in comradely fashion, and off we went, wending our way in leisurely fashion towards the projected park, me feeling all the while quietly confident of the outcome of the excursion, supremely assured that the brown bottle in my beach-bag held an elixir that would impress my companion with my evident sophistication and devastating cosmopolitanism. The whole effect could only be a *little* diminished or diluted by the couple of old toothmugs thoughtfully loaned for the occasion by an ever-benevolent Royal Hotel management.

Nowhere in the Italian Gardens appeared to please my poppet . . . too many other strollers admiring flowers and fountains perhaps. By the time we had transferred to, and traversed, the Valley Gardens dusk was nigh, dew might have fallen and the inviting grassy slopes be too damp for a momentary sit-down or a rest. My inamorata's final choice of an ideal location where we might pause to sit and chat, ponder the problems of the busy world, was odd – quite disconcerting in fact and, ultimately, quite off-putting.

The scene for this delightful dalliance (amatory or not, I still knew not – but continued in high hopes) lay beneath the concealing canopy afforded by the foliage of an enormous hawthorn bush – a relatively secret place, but alarmingly close to a public street, a thoroughfare which carried a myriad crowd of gently perambulating holiday-makers. Eminently curious, and much worse, was the fact that this bushy bower was diametrically opposite the front door of my admired one's parents' home, their boarding house (I forgot to point out Ethel's catering trade connections). A cynic might well have supposed that she knew the place of old, having visited it upon earlier occasions; she appeared to relax as we crawled through the encircling nettles and long grass to gain entry into her haven.

Sadly, and somewhat to my chagrin, Ethel did not seem to share my anxious enthusiasm for the hastily and clumsily poured (and largely spilled) aperitif, precursor to our deliberations – or, indeed, for anything else. Lighting a cigarette, she became, if that were possible, more monosyllabic than before, but appeared to indicate that I might now apply myself to our mutual entertainment, to the long awaited (and long dreamt of) task of her seduction, so I began . . .

There were no handbooks regarding the arts of love, no manuals on lovemaking, in those days or, at any rate, none of which I knew or to which I had access. Still, I took myself to be a reasonably alert lad, a relatively rapid learner, and as keen as mustard to do my best to get to grips with this particular and much anticipated challenge. I still wistfully believe that, under happier circumstances, I might have enjoyed a minor triumph, merited beginner's laurels for rough, makeshift enterprise and for the assiduous and industrious application of new-found skills; might have felt mildly satisfied that an inkling of some of the mysteries of 'life' had been bestowed upon me.

It was not to be; matters did not quite work out as I had so fervently wished. The odalisque lay on her back, languidly puffing on

Craven A after Craven A, obviously and obliviously careless as to anything that I might contrive to enact upon her graciously offered form. But, *somehow*, romance was not upon that evening's air. Disregarding the addiction to smoking (something to which I was already mildly antipathetic), the proximity of our trysting place to her childhood home (it was possible to discern the outlines of a teddy bear in the window of her attic room across the road) and the constant slamming of the boarding house's door contrived to have a singularly detumescent effect.

All experience has its value – so they say; I am perfectly prepared to accept that the aphorism is true. Something in the way of pertinent knowledge must have come my way that sultry night in June . . . but it set back my enthusiasm for fino sherry (Tio Pepe in particular) for many years afterwards. In the short term I consoled my damaged vanity with soothing draughts of bitter and, from time to time, a glass of roughish wine.

With the end of the two years' pre-clinical training at Leeds Dental School my life and times as a waiter finished too. After four hectic summer seasons spent working in hotels, I had learned an astonishing amount about petty pilfering, something of how to deal with difficult or recalcitrant hotel guests, a little of the art of self-preservation in awkward situations, and the bare fact of the existence of good wine. On the other hand, my comprehension of such esoteric matters as anatomy or physiology was shaky, to say the least – my grasp of either being far less than my mentors might have wished – but, somehow, I was allowed to start my third university year as a clinical student. From then on summer vacations consisted of a mere three hard-fought-for weeks that precluded vacation employment . . . so the catering trade lost an enthusiastic novice.

There was one minor reversion to my former *métier*, however. Midway through the autumn term I happened to run into a former colleague (on licensed premises, of course: The Turk's Head – still going strong, I am delighted to report), 'Old John', who spent the winter months (during which the Royal was closed completely) with an equally antique sister in a suburb of the city. My bemoaning my usual lack of funds gave the old man an idea. His own income was supplemented by an occasional night's employment by a firm of outside caterers who frequently needed 'extra ducks', waiters hired on a casual basis: would I be interested if he were to use his good offices on my behalf, put in a word for me? Certainly I would!

So it was that, for two or three evenings a week, I would make time-consuming, complicated permutations of bus rides to previously unheard of parts of the West Riding, to Morley Town Hall, Keighley Town Hall, or some other smoke-blackened monument to the civic virtue of nineteenth-century industrialists. There, in the draughty and always wildly inconvenient corridors of the building, would have been set up a clutch of makeshift mobile stoves employed in a valiant attempt to de-congeal some institutional soup, or to breathe reluctant warmth into whatever dish the particular party had selected. In this unlikely Dantesque setting I would team up with my evening's companions for the work ahead.

What 'Old John' had failed to mention was the alarming fact that he and I would be the only *male* 'extra ducks', a brace of drakes as it were: all the rest were women. Four years in the hotel world – a milieu never noted for its gentleness or decorum – had done little to prepare me for these harridans. I had never heard, neither have I since, such vile, imprecation-rich, profanity-punctuated vulgarity as from those ladies' lips. Whoever coined 'fishwife' as a description of forthright, uninhibited stridency must have led a sheltered life – 'Yorkshire waitress' would make the proper epithet.

I was terrified; with good reason too. I became the rallying point, the butt, for all their lively humour, and was probably quite lucky not to lose my trousers. When I did not burst into tears, even managed a feeble riposte or two, and when it was noted that I was sufficiently competent to cope with my share of distributing the feast to whichever expectant throng of masons or benevolent policemen awaited sustenance in the body of the hall (no wine there, or not a lot – pitchers and pint mugs of Tetley's bitter furnished those tables), all became well, and I was grudgingly accepted as a rather bizarre but well-intentioned fellow toiler. 'Rough diamonds with hearts of gold' is the slightly mixed metaphor that ideally summed up those hard-working, cheerful women, and I thoroughly enjoyed the warmth of their camaraderie for a month or so. In the end the complications and length of the travelling, the spectacularly poor pay (always a particular grievance of the vocation) and, most of all, the strongly worded advice of my tutors that I should pay at least fleeting attention to my textbooks put paid to my unusual apprenticeship in catering.

Apprenticeship in Teeth and Wine

For the next three and a half years I succeeded in being reasonably assiduous at my studies – sufficiently so as eventually to qualify, which I celebrated by heading south. I became the assistant in the dental practice of an agreeable enough man who really should have been a full-time sailor, instead of three-quarters mariner, one-quarter old-school dentist – even his dental unit, a crude home-made job, looked more like a ship's binnacle than any sort of scientific instrument. Exmouth was a pleasant place for a first job, situated on the South Devon coast where the estuary of the Exe meets the English Channel, backed by rolling wooded Devon hills; I liked the location, and rather planned to settle down. The theory was that I should be given full partnership within a year or so, but it quickly became clear that I was merely the present incumbent of the assistantship, inadequately paid to hold the fort (and forceps) while my senior colleague passed the daylight hours down at the dock, fiddling away at interminable repairs that his mini-flotilla of four boats endlessly required, or merrily cruised the Channel coast in a splendid two-masted steel Dutch ketch. Apparently many assistants had arrived at the seedy premises in Exeter Road, all presumably as imbued with optimism as I; none had ever got the merest whisper of a firm invitation into the promised partnership; all had eventually left in disillusion, after several years of cynical exploitation at the hands of the wily mariner and his frightful spouse.

This four-square chunky female was the only person who appeared to have the ability to exert any influence upon, or to disconcert, my employer – which she frequently did, by shouting. A former Wren (it was tempting to suppose a stoker), it was rumoured that, once upon a time, her stentorian tones could be clearly heard from one end of Scapa Flow to the other. The combination of Jack's patent lack of sincerity over future closer collaboration and the malevolent disapproval of his lovely lady ensured my early departure. I saw the warning signs of potential frustration earlier than my predecessors, and departed within the year.

Whenever possible, I had, when funds permitted, continued my researches into wine right through studenthood. One major investment was the bottle of Château Ducru Beaucaillou 1955 that set me back the heady sum of 12s 6d in a small emporium behind Leeds City Varieties music hall; but I cannot recall the flavour of the wine. Probably the outlay of such a large proportion of my grant precluded its objective appreciation – nothing could have lived up to such a price! In Exmouth, with a regular (though always modest) income, I set about trying to repair the glaring defects in my vinous knowledge, buying bottles and books, drinking the contents of one and imbibing the lore of the other in roughly equal measure. One particular source supplied much of both valuable commodities – good wine and excellent information.

Once, when I attempted to honour my enormous debt to Gerald Asher, I quickly learned that I had unwittingly stirred up a hornets' nest of outraged indignation from still sensitive victims of his financial demise at the fag-end of the 1960s. Mr Asher had a wine company that, in its earliest days, rejoiced in the title of the Professional and Businessmen's Wine Vaults Limited – later transmuted into the simpler, less grandiloquent, Wine Vaults Limited. Although Wine Vaults possessed exactly that invaluable commodity – extensive and capacious cellars below Tower Hill – and sold wine to calling customers, one of its chief distinctions lay in Mr Asher being an early pioneer of mail order wine supply; another is that, on top of a list of a careful selection of France's classic wines, burgundy and claret, he had assembled an impressive collection of rare and esoteric wines, discovered in some of the most obscure corners of viticultural France. Just how these liquid treasures had been prised from the *caves* of French growers, notoriously suspicious of strangers, I do not know – I little realized then how extraordinarily difficult *that* particular sleight of hand can prove; but here, on general sale, were unheard-of curiosities, such as Irancy (a little-known anachronism from a tiny *vignoble* that is a relic of vineyards that once extended from Auxerre to Chablis) or Lirac from the Southern Rhône. A revealing feature of the Asher lists of the 1960s is that his modest selection of Rhône wines was not denominated by grower – simply by their generic titles, which shows (as does the careless lack of attention accorded the Rhône in the Royal's *carte aux vins*) how shockingly disregarded those wines then were.

In addition to the novelty of this choice of product, this remarkable man wrote (and still does) like a literate, wine-loving angel; the regular wine lists were marvels of enthusiasm and models of pertinent prose. I still jealously guard all my copies of these brochures, and value them enormously – the only problem being that re-reading them completely inhibits me from putting pen to paper for days and days, so well written are the essays they contain.

So education in wine and its literature continued apace – a great deal of it by courtesy of the amazing Mr Asher. Like many a slightly perplexed Wine Vaults customer, I purchased wines of which I had never previously heard and (mostly) liked them. Examples of more classic wines also arrived in Exeter Road; included in their number were a couple of bottles of a very particular burgundy that seemed to cost a fortune: a Morcy-Saint Denis, Clos de la Roche 1959 at 25s 3d made by the (I now realize) legendary Armand Rousseau. Both bottles of this precious fluid were broached for some significant celebration . . . and I did not *like* the wine: I loathed the stuff in fact. Never much of a hand at the high-flown, colourful similes that so many wine writers seem to have at their fingertips, the best that I could summon up for this major disappointment was that the pungent liquid resembled nothing so much as the smell and flavour of over-well-hung game, of rotting flesh. Upon my telling Asher of my concern at this oddity, he courteously asked me to send back one of the barely touched bottles for his considered appraisal. The charming letter accompanying a credit note had an extremely puzzled tenor: the wine had been judged as excellent, even superb (with due allowance made for any oxidation in transit). Sadly, the Vaults had no more stock with which to replace the criticized bottles, hence the credit note. The lesson was salutary; I am now convinced that I had had the privilege to encounter what were, quite possibly, the greatest bottles of burgundy in my life, but had foolishly spurned the opportunity; that tremendously rich concentration of flavours had alarmed my inexperienced senses. I would dearly like to relive the moment – in the light of twenty-five years' drinking experience! Still, the incident served as a much-needed lesson in humility, and prepared me for a subsequent illuminating incident. I also trust that my appreciation of Asher's tolerance, in what must have been infuriating circumstances, has given me at least a degree of the same forbearance and understanding when *my* customers complain or query.

While Gerald Asher was introducing the likes of me to fascinating, outlandish wines, something was going sadly awry with the commercial structure of his enterprise. A pioneering scheme, in which the Wine Vaults (for a reasonable rental) undertook the long-term guardianship of customers' paid reserves within its spacious cellars near the Tower of London, was well received, quickly and enthusiastically taken up . . . which is why the subsequent abrupt financial demise of the company occasioned such astonishing reverberations. Eventually the vociferously disputed ownership of the thousands of already purchased cartons that crammed the Wine Vaults' cellars was decided upon in draconian fashion, hinging upon a legal technicality, a judicial nicety, that infuriated the innocent supposed owners of the wine. If the paid-for reserved cartons had been subdivided into separate parcels that represented each individual purchaser's property then, said the learned judge, those individuals might have removed their cases of wine, without let or hindrance, at their earliest convenience. Unfortunately, though each and every transaction figured clearly in the ledgers, and was clearly set out in the accounts, the wines themselves had been physically stored in stacks representing their type and place of origin – a logical enough system, one might reasonably have supposed. The judge thought otherwise: this method, he pronounced, was a different kettle of fish (or vat of wine) altogether, and promptly awarded title of the goods in question to the official receiver. At the subsequent dispersal auction, held in the Beaver Hall, one witnessed the extraordinary spectacle of erstwhile Wine Vaults clients purchasing a favoured wine for the second time around. Small wonder that my article, making complimentary and grateful reference to Mr Asher, should arouse the extreme ire of such unfortunates – even after many years.

Not being in the position of a major purchaser (receiving and consuming my modest dozens with avidity and remarkable rapidity), the débâcle affected me little. This wonderful source of interesting and reasonably priced wines inevitably dried up and, a further concomitant of catastrophe, so did the excellent articles on good wine which had given me and so many others such guidance and such pleasure. A further negative consequence was that the Wine Vaults' fall from grace coincided approximately with the birth of my own wine venture; it really was a most inauspicious moment in which to attempt to woo the British wine-buying public. However, no matter what his commercial indiscretions or shortcomings, at Gerald Asher's feet should be laid at least some of the blame and responsibility for steering me deeper into the world of wine.

Life in Exmouth was a curious amalgam of what seemed remarkably like an unfair workload and periods of relative calm. Wednesday afternoons were particularly peaceful because they were the half-days when I was required to attend the practice's branch surgery in neighbouring Budleigh Salterton – then as now one of the most charmingly old-fashioned seaside towns imaginable. I usually took as work companion the prettier of the two dental nurses (nowadays referred to as 'chairside assistants': I cannot imagine wherein lies the difference), and off we would drive along the coast to Budleigh.

Branch surgery afternoons were highlights of an otherwise too action-packed week. The premises were above a second-hand book-shop in an unprepossessing redbrick terrace of poky postwar shops very near the station. The door sorely needed a coat of paint, the stairs were steep, dimly lit and dingy, and the waiting room was the epitome of grim discomfort. The only available reading material consisted of tatty, dog-eared copies of yachting magazines five years out of date; the surgery was equipped (or wildly under-equipped) with rusting relics of instruments that might have been (and probably were) filched from some dental scrapyard in the dim and distant past. All sane patients of the practice wisely preferred the expense and inconvenience of a bus trip to Exmouth – where the reading material was a year or so more up to date, and the ship's binnacle had a reassuring rustic charm, redolent as it was of patient handicraft. The homeliness of the Exmouth premises far outweighed the historical fascination of the satellite surgery. At Budleigh Salterton the patients stayed away in droves, achieving a near-total boycott so, on Wednesday afternoons, I could quietly study wine lists and plot out complex graphs of comparative claret prices, while the nurse sat in a springless armchair, attending to her fingernails.

This agreeable routine was varied only when, on the infrequent hot summer afternoons, I would amble the half-mile to the seafront, don swimming trunks, pick my way gingerly across the large pebbles that pass for Budleigh's beach, and immerse myself into the chilly embrace of the English Channel. After an energetic sprint from shore, I would recuperate upon a raft thoughtfully moored there for that purpose by a caring council. The 'chairside assistant' and I had devised a simple but effective system for use in the rare and unlikely event of some misguided and foolhardy potential patient hale enough to manage the stairs presenting him or herself in the waiting room: the obliging girl would leg it along to the foreshore and wave a coloured surgery towel to alert me to the need for urgent attendance upon the dentally sick.

Mostly it was the wine lists, though, that held me in thrall. Laboriously, I would make intricate comparisons of cost and, after due planning, decide upon a possible purchase. In those days I was so devoted to my emergent passion that I actually kept a cellar book (well, exercise book), so that I am able to reconstruct some of my amazing wine-buying coups. There is nothing so painfully irritating as having to read about wonderful vintages of long ago that were once available at enviably accessible prices. Such is the criticism that is frequently made against the most celebrated cellar book of all: Professor George Saintsbury's *Notes on a Cellar Book*, originally published in 1920 and still going strong in an umpteenth edition. Not numbered among the critics of that work, I must confess that I love the book; the author was doubtless a crusty, pedantic old scholar, but he loved his wine and succeeded in conveying his devotion with elegant wit and strong conviction. While I have no intention of aspiring to the great man's level of enthusiastic enumeration of long-gone bottles, the opportunity to arouse others' envy at my great good fortune at being around at the right moment, coupled with an insatiable urge to buy, is I confess quite irresistible.

The early 1960s were a period of great change in the wine industry, and a time when bargains were to be had – if one was prepared to search them out. A complete list of the liquid treasures that I then acquired would require a disproportionate amount of space, and be boringly unreadable to boot. Most of these fortunate finds came in small lots, usually two or three bottles, but every so often a more numerous cache might be encountered. A chance visit to a firm of, I seem to recall, licensed grocers in the far-away foreign territory of Brighton proved to be a momentarily rich vein; thence came seven bottles of Latour 1949, for 43s each; a few weeks later (a mortgage arranged) the same quantity of Château Margaux 1945 followed suit, at 48s a bottle (it may help to put matters into perspective to remember that the same wine went for £5 12s 6d at Christie's a few years later); the brace of Château Rausan Ségla 1945 were a positive snip at 23s each. I must have cleared Messrs Edlin's shelves in the two brief sorties, or failed to augment the mortgage, because the name does not recur thereafter.

The Château Margaux proved to be a disappointment upon first examination – much sterner stuff than I had previously come across. The story went (and does so yet) that Margaux 1945 had the lurking potential to develop into being one of the greatest wines of the century, but was biding its time in tannin-stuffed disguise, waiting to reveal eventual magnificence. Whether my original lack of appreciation stemmed from my poor stage of development or that of the wine would be difficult to judge. A subsequent bottle was pretty convincing; the three that remain present a problem: how much longer should I hang on before decanting their costly contents?

Because costly they became. Soon after my debut as a wine merchant, a young neighbour, not especially noted for his intellectual stature but who occasionally bought a small quantity of what he amusingly referred to as my 'cheapo plonk', confided a dilemma. His late, wine-loving father had departed in such haste as to have left eight cases – ninety-six bottles! – of Château Margaux 1945 in his cellar. My informant had casually uncorked three bottles, one after another, hoping to find something pleasant with which to wash down some spaghetti Bolognese. Appalled by the horridness of the dark-hued beverage (I remembered my own first taste), he refrained from pouring the contents of *all* the bottles down the sink, only because he suddenly thought of me.

He thought me to be a 'sporting sort of cove'; would I be prepared to take the ninety-three remaining bottles off his hands, on the principle that at least a few of them might prove to be drinkable, for a case or two of 'cheapo plonk'? With the clearest image before my eyes of the £2,000 or so that a case of the distasteful wine had fetched at a recent London auction, I rapidly wrestled with my conscience, until some attendant guardian angel pushed me over on to the side of rectitude and honour. When young Hugh had been made to understand just what a sale room *was*, had been made aware that some such establishments actually specialized in wine, I proceeded to elucidate to him the dizzy price horizons that might possibly be anticipated – at which point he asked to sit down.

At his slightly incoherent behest, I telephoned an old friend in the trade. The then chief wine auctioneer at Sotheby's, Patrick Grubb, became as incoherent as my visitor when the news had finally sunk in, but eventually he confirmed my suggested price range. Feeling uncommonly virtuous, I ushered my customer off the premises. Hugh telephoned me that evening – to thank me once again, as I presumed. But no; an immense and overwhelming sense of filial piety and pride had overcome the lad. He had had no idea that his revered sire could have been so amazingly astute as to lay down such precious stuff. Upon what he called 'mature reflection', Hugh was quite certain where his course should lie; London sale rooms would never see his unexpected inheritance – he proposed to drink the lot himself.

This was a period when small independent wine merchants, mostly of long-standing reputation, were being absorbed by the major companies – particularly the larger brewery conglomerates – at an alarming rate of knots. Small caches of surplus stock were liable suddenly to manifest themselves upon the market. More significant, amalgamations were subject to the accountants' whims, and their ideas of 'rationalization'; these slide-rule magicians ruled as absolutely out of the question the maintenance of vast stockpiles of fine wine that had been accumulated by well-known and sufficiently wealthy firms, which had perhaps been more strongly endowed with carefree and enthusiastic buyers than with shrewd marketing men.

Harveys' monthly remnant bulletins were circulated on a restricted-recipient basis. A friend had access to this valuable document which was an eagerly awaited hunting field. Always noted as a breeding bed of a whole generation of gifted wine trade personalities (Harry Waugh and Michael Broadbent for two), it was said to be the unrivalled opportunities to taste fine wine that brought on these men. More probably, it was the chance of so much exposure to the product that attracted so much talent to Bristol in the first place. I am extremely thankful that the company, then just lately taken over by Showerings of Shepton Mallet, extended to me the same generous opportunity to explore the higher strata of good claret and fine burgundy by virtue of the agreeably low-priced beauties that studded the keenly anticipated bin-end list.

Château Gazin 1952 and Trottevieille 1955, both in halves, at 8s 6d and 7s respectively – my goodness, they were good; the half bottles of Bristol-bottled Lynch Bages 1953 – 4s 6d a time, the most splendid accompaniment to a supper of cheese on toast, and possibly the greatest 'steal' of all. A case of Château Cos d'Estournel 1961 cost 21s a bottle, but I have yet to open a bottle; the list goes on and on. Some ancient Madeira, a bottle each of Malmsey and of Sercial, both of the vintage 1871, at 60s and 45s; some most delicious white burgundy, Meursault les Charmes 1957, at 5s 10d each (*bottles*, not halves)! Four bottles of Volnay: General Muteau 1952 from the Hospices de Beaune at 20s – but I cannot recall its flavour, having made the usual error of not noting my reaction when the bottles were consumed – and so on. I was early a 'claret man'; not that I have ever been so negligent as not to demand my share of any halfway decent burgundy whenever given the chance.

Only one wine from this bounteous flow of Harveys' remnants ever gave me cause for concern, and that was the Château Figeac 1955, of which I had been fortunate enough to acquire a dozen. At 14s a bottle, it was, while it lasted, the cheapest wine in the shoe-cupboard cellar of my flat – cheaper even than a moderate Beaujolais. Having taken far more than my fair share of the bottle I opened on the night of the wine's arrival, a second (tried a few days later) seemed distinctly less palatable, while the third (consumed within the week) produced alarming symptoms of nausea and gastric distress. In retrospect I can only guess that my long-suffering faculties, both gustatory and intellectual, were protesting at such a savage onslaught, an ordeal by the richly complex factors making up an obviously important wine.

Purchases for more day-to-day drinking came from the ever-obliging Gerald Asher, or from the Wine Society (or the International Exhibition Co-operative Wine Society, to give this organization its full and proper title), which I had joined when entry cost £5.

Founded by a group of wine-loving professional men at the time of a Great Exhibition in 1874, the Wine Society must have been the earliest exponent of mail order wine distribution, in which method of wine trading it continues today – with conspicuous success. About this time, the serendipitous finding of rare vintages at absurdly low prices gradually began to falter: the wine wells were beginning to run dry. A wine shop in nearby Exeter, Davy's (contiguous to the ancient White Hart Inn), provided what must have been one of the last of the notably memorable bargains. I had never previously met Château Cheval Blanc – in *any* vintage, let alone that of 1953. Twelve bottles multiplied by 37s 6d came to £22 10s; I certainly could not afford such a major investment but, equally, was not prepared to pass up what I correctly felt to be a unique opportunity to investigate a famous wine in a memorable vintage at relatively modest cost. It was fortunate that I did stump up the cash: the first bottle of that case of majestic Cheval Blanc was destined to change my entire concept and comprehension of wine.

My first daughter, Katy, was born during the evening of 5 November 1963 at Exeter's maternity hospital. When the sergeant-major of a midwife had ejected me from the ward after the briefest glimpse of mother and child, I drove the fifteen miles to Exmouth in a state of great elation. Two female hitchhikers who had flagged me down clearly thought that I was raging drunk, or mad, and suddenly recollected that their appointment was in the village we were then passing through, not Exmouth after all. The brightly exploding rockets of bonfire parties illuminating the sky served as a highly appropriate accompaniment to my euphoric mood.

Back home in Exeter Road a young couple who were my particular friends (and wine enthusiasts too) awaited my return with a simple picnic supper and a bottle of champagne. I do not remember a great deal about that impromptu party, other than that Joan Sutherland contributed to our happy state of mind with a spirited rendering of the sleepwalking scene from *Lucia di Lammermoor* at a volume sufficient to put on bedroom lights in houses opposite. The champagne all too rapidly consumed, I reached for a bottle of the recently purchased Château Cheval Blanc, and smartly replenished our empty glasses.

It was not drinking the wine itself that did the trick – I was far too preoccupied with happy chatter to pay it due attention; it was the little that remained at the bottom of the quickly drained goblet, the dregs, that suddenly caught my attention, stopped me short in excited mid-conversation. Unthinkingly, I had sniffed the virtually empty glass, and was arrested by what assailed my nostrils. For the very first time I became electrifyingly aware of the magnificence and splendour that a wine's aroma might evince. At that moment, a large number of hitherto disparate elements seemed to fall into perfect place; in that instant, what had been several years' not inconsiderable enthusiasm was translated into a positive obsession with the delights of fine wine.

I suppose that there had always been a strong 'emperor's new clothes' element about my perception of wine until that moment of revelation: I had been trying too hard to find in each glassful exactly what the literature said should be there. The great joy of truly sensing for myself, for the very first time, the marvellous aspects that a magnificent wine of a great vintage can hold when at something approaching maturity is perhaps understandable if thus explained.

Professional Plunge

Before departing the undoubted charms of Exmouth and the more debatable pleasures of sailor Jack's unusual establishment, I planned my next move with a care worthy of a wartime operations room. I made a survey of the deployment of dental manpower in a number of small towns scattered throughout what might loosely be referred to as the West Country. My researches involved careful inquiries made in the course of brief visits to the selected targets. Public houses proved a remarkable source of information (and it was possible to check out the local brew at the same time); the well-timed proffering of a half-pint of the indigenous ale seemed to lubricate tongues with impressive speed, so that I was able to garner invaluable statistics regarding the reputations and waiting lists of any resident dental surgeons. Some of the lurid stories that came my way were worthy of a book of their own.

Eliminating several other close contenders for the benefit of my professional favours, I made a final choice. Gillingham, a not particularly attractive (an extensive fire in the seventeenth century ravaged the buildings; the damage was compounded by the subsequent establishment of a brickworks, the product of which boasts a strikingly virulent hue) but a bustling and friendly small town in North Dorset, very near to the Somerset and Wiltshire borders, won the contest – or lost, as a few unkind recipients of my best dental efforts have been sometimes heard to quip.

One old practitioner, who had spent forty years and more wielding his art upon the populace, had recently retired without nominating a successor. Originally he had been a dental mechanic, a maker of dentures and appliances, until he had picked up some idea of the senior trade by a sort of apprenticeship, prior to an Act of 1926 which insisted upon at least a modicum of formal dental training before a dentist was let loose upon the world at large. Pre-dating the Act by quite a while, the old boy had served the town for a very long time, but in his later working life reverted to his earliest occupation of making false teeth, so his full retirement had not been much noticed by the community.

Another, only marginally less ancient, had a practice along the High Street; a painter *manqué*, half his week was spent in cycling around the surrounding countryside, paintbox and palette strapped to the handlebars, while the balance of his time was employed in performing a curious form of dentistry which he perpetrated with the aid of a treadle-machine drill. Otherwise the field was clear.

Practices in the three neighbouring towns were rather more conventionally, even scientifically, organized, but were patently not coping with the nine-month waiting lists of less than enthusiastic would-be patients. Some of these new-found colleagues were more reputable than others; one particularly celebrated local dentist was positively notorious.

Some years earlier he had carelessly mislaid an eye – in a pub brawl – but it did not appear to have curbed his interest in those places of entertainment. It was common knowledge that the only truly ideal times of appointment lay within the brief span between 11.40 a.m. and 12.30 p.m. Any earlier than that, popular and widely disseminated opinion was that the unnerving Cyclopean eye might not focus quite as perfectly as a naturally apprehensive prospective client might ideally wish. A pub adjacent to the surgery flung open its portals at precisely 11 a.m., seemingly to welcome the arrival of the parched practitioner – it was generally understood that he found that enamel (human enamel, be it understood) dust always created a powerful thirst. The other alternative, a surgical mask, was thought impractical and far too constraining. With dry throat adequately slaked, the dentist was known to put in a veritably inspired performance for just about an hour, after which, the townsfolk felt, his later excursions for refreshments had a discernibly deleterious effect upon his accuracy.

With the usual young man's difficulty in presenting a façade of financial credibility, it proved pretty difficult to muster the essential funds with which to buy a substantial Victorian end-of-terrace house in the middle of the town.

The elderly manager of the more imposing of the town's two banks, who refused (with great reluctance, or so he said) urgently needed borrowing facilities, was later thought by some citizens to have been perhaps imprudent in having sought my professional advice once I had scraped together sufficient cash (from a number of widely disparate sources) to buy and open up the surgery. A few days after what had been an innocuous enough session in my dental chair, the poor fellow was found slumped lifeless across his desk by a counter clerk. Fortunately, the greater part of town opinion inclined to the belief that the two occurrences were not necessarily interlinked. I had originally anticipated that it might take several years to establish the practice on a satisfactorily commercial footing and to consolidate its reputation; in the event, and to my relieved suprise, I found myself fully booked up for the month ahead within eight days of opening up, in May 1964, and the situation remained pretty well the same for the next two decades.

Completely coincidentally, the surgery had been that of my retired denture-making predecessor – as a magnificent dawn-of-the-century fully electrified dental unit proclaimed (I have always regretted my negligence in failing to offer this splendid machine to the Science Museum, but was glad of its scrap value at the time). Immediate and total redecoration was essential. It was not necessary to hazard a guess at the aeons that had passed since the last coat of paint: the faded state of the bloodstains on the ceiling above the well-worn, leather-upholstered, equally museum-piece chair showed that some of them were obviously of ancient date. It was in fact evident that the 'decorations' were original, dating from the construction of the building during the last years of the nineteenth century: the hallway's gloomy wallpaper was *not* a latterday facsimile of some Victorian model; it was quite definitely the real thing! What seemed like dozens of coats of light-coloured emulsion paint, designed to ease the Stygian gloom, failed to obliterate the paper's awesomely intricate design; those early papers were printed with arsenic-impregnated dyes that lifted straight through all vain attempts at concealment. New wallpaper was unavoidable.

I could not afford to buy much in the way of wine for several years, so heavy were the debts incurred in setting up the practice. An extremely venerable treadle-machine drill (even more antique than that in regular use at my painter rival's establishment along the High Street) came to light in an attic cupboard; later I was sorry about its hurried sale to a collector of dental curios but, at the time, the £5 the object fetched seemed most timely. However, I *did* hang on to the copy of Krafft-Ebing's *Psychopathia Sexualis* which I found in the same hiding place, discreetly wrapped in a plain brown envelope: until then I had not realized that the old dentist had held such a wide-ranging interest in matters scientific.

I must have looked absurdly young in those days; presumably younger than my twenty-four years. New patients quite frequently expressed a preference to be treated by my father. As he had been a journalist all his working life, I felt disinclined to distract him from painting the surgery's front door – a task which he had generously undertaken; instead, when other persuasion failed, out of the desk drawer would come my degree certificate, for the edification of the most irredeemably doubting of the customers. An itinerant navvy must have been extra grateful for the removal of an aching molar; on his way out to the reception area, he slipped me two half-crowns, with the muttered advice that I should not bring the incident to the boss's attention. As it would only have confused the excellent fellow if I had attempted to explain to him that my apprentice days were over, I quietly pocketed the coins.

It is a most regrettable state of affairs that a profession such as dentistry should be the victim of an educational system where the emphasis frequently lies more upon the academic than the practical. Also at that stage, certainly my own training school, and probably others, suffered from woefully inadequate funding: our initial experience of drilling teeth was with a treadle machine – I would have been perfectly capable of operating the antique that I sold! When I qualified, I was one of only three people in my year who had had the good fortune to use an air turbine drill – the method then universal in any halfway self-respecting surgery in the land. Truthfully, I started my dental career with almost everything to learn about professional life in the real world: my apprenticeship was *far* from over. At this point I recognized the value of the multifarious experience I had gained in hotel life; experience which was to stand me in good stead.

Eventually, my economy began to show signs of marked improvement. Wine buying once again became a possibility. After a couple of years spent camping in the rooms above the surgery, I moved to a four-square simple but attractive house hidden in a complex of narrow lanes on the Dorset–Wiltshire border, just a mile from Mere.

Like most houses in the district, Hinckes Mill House had the severe handicap (for a drinking man) of having no cellar. Built for the occupancy of the manager of an eighteenth-century silk mill (converted to a farmstead a century or so ago) a little way down the hill, the absence of that nigh-on essential domestic office, a storehouse for bottles of wine, probably owed more to the temperate appetites of the original manager (or of the Duchy of Cornwall, founder of the silk mill) than to the terrain, as the house lay well above the water table – the normal reason for failing to provide a cellar in those parts. However, a roomy cupboard beneath the stairs could hold a reasonable number of bottles in tolerably good conditions once it had been adequately insulated against the sudden fluctuations of temperature with which a normal domestic central heating system so often endangers wine. This makeshift cellar served me well – until the garage had eventually to be brought into play.

The question was with what to fill the neatly arranged rows of bins? An indecently high proportion of the older wines I had so diligently sought out in Devon days had long since been sipped – or sometimes quaffed. At the time I had started up in Gillingham, my doctor brother, ten years my senior, had given himself and us a scare. Having worked as a doctor in a succession of exotic countries, America, New Zealand and Barbados, Michael had recently contracted to look after the medical needs of the employees of a British construction company that was laying an oil pipeline from the Sahara to the sea, across the deserts, forests and mountains of Algeria. Indeed, I had obtained the original set of forceps for the new surgery from my brother's latest employers: the company had paid me to fly out to Algeria to make a 2,000-mile taxi ride right across the country, taking out as I went the offending teeth of roughneck pipeline builders on hotel balconies in the cities, on mountain tops, under palm trees, in orange groves, by oases and by sand dunes. I seemed to have forgotten to return the dental instruments when my two-week taxi ride was over. With very few exceptions, the local wines were terrible. Every bottle in the land carried the same vintage label, 1959; it relieved the constructors' monotonous existence a little when the whole of the country moved on to 1961, or so my brother said.

When Michael turned up in Dorset completely unexpectedly and unannounced, it was obvious that something must be drastically wrong, and so it was. In usual medical fashion, he had at first neglected to register, and then to take seriously, certain worrying symptoms. By the time he had consulted a medical colleague, the carcinoma was fairly advanced. An immediate repatriation and the speedy surgical removal of the tumour at St Mary's Hospital, Paddington, was to be followed by some months of deep irradiation with the object of eliminating any secondary growths. He was to be allowed to spend weekends in the country with me.

The period that followed this earthquake of an announcement was very strange and, at times, curiously happy. As the weeks passed, Michael become more and more debilitated by the treatment – a common consequence of heavy irradiation, we were told. With his appetite diminished to the point of near-extinction, the consultant, evidently worried, urged his patient to indulge himself with whatever luxury might tempt his fancy and, as an added inducement, reminded him that it was perfectly acceptable for him to imbibe a moderate amount of *red* wine; *red* wine would be in no way deleterious; *red* wine would not impair or inhibit the efficacy of the treatment.

So, every Friday evening, an increasingly emaciated Michael would alight from the London train, accompanied by a Fortnum's bag that might contain anything from *foie gras* to caviare (quite often both). With the supposedly secret, but tacitly shared, awareness that these poignant reunions might possibly prove to be of short duration, we quietly washed down Mr Fortnum's delicacies with the finest red wines in my possession. As weekend succeeded weekend, we became conversant with the nuances of such touchstones of excellence as Château Mouton Rothschild 1953, Lafite 1953, Latour 1949 and many, many others. Then, as the contents of my wine store inexorably diminished, Michael began to show signs of gradually returning to health, the semblance of a cure. Of course those wondrous bottles played no part in his slow recovery, but their contents had certainly helped to assuage our sadness, and had often made us light-hearted. It was the happiest of sacrifices; those nectareous wines had mitigated our underlying forebodings wonderfully well. In due course my brother flew back to North Africa . . . and the wine cupboard was astonishingly bare. It was time for some repair work.

Normal contact had been maintained with various aforementioned suppliers, Messrs Asher, *et al.*, but in extremely timely fashion a new and rather curious organization came my way. The Private Wine Buyers' Society must have been eminently amateur – its wine lists were something of a joke, duplicated at they were on some superannuated Gestetner. With the eye of faith (or thirst) it was just about possible to make out the wares on offer through the chiaroscuro created by an ancient but lovingly preserved stencil. The principle behind the Private Wine Buyers' Society was an original one, and most appealing to someone with an empty cellar. The main commodity on offer was a variety of wines, furnished by a handful of rather uncomfortably pseudonymous *négociants*, wine brokers, available to all in anything from a hogshead to a bottle. The idea of the bottles worried me a little; there seemed a distinct possibility that they *might* be the surplus, or the rejects, of the home bottling activities of the officials of the club. That was the whole *raison d'être* of the Society; its underlying purpose was to encourage the bottling up of casks.

The concept was irresistible. Two reasonably wine-keen friends were promptly co-opted on to my team, and some wine was ordered – a generic Saint Emilion for starters. We thought a hogshead too much of an initial challenge, perhaps a little greedy: so we settled for a 'library' cask, a neat little wooden keg, weighing in at 150 pounds, and containing the approximate equivalent of six dozen bottles.

Two months later a cask sample was delivered from Southampton Docks, where our baby now resided. We did not know what to do with the sample (though we admired the professionalism of the touch), so we drank it. It did not taste very nice but, after all, the wine was still extremely young, and could only improve with age. The keg itself followed the sample admirably promptly. It looked extremely small, lying there on a brandreth in the kitchen. Next evening the three of us assembled and, with remarkably little spillage, succeeded in transferring wine from barrel to bottles. An unexpected bonus of the venture was that the contents were equivalent to six and a half dozen bottles (although there were a lot more 70 cl bottles about in those days, which may well have affected the situation). Only seventy-two bottles had been commandeered for that evening's activity (the liberation of bottles was, of course, part of the appeal of the whole thing: you had to *drink* wine so as to have empty bottles to fill, and so on . . . marvellous, really). We were decisive, and acted fast: rather than let the surplus oxidize overnight and (we were certain) spoil, we felt constrained to consume the balance with promptitude. It began to seem quite potable after all.

And as alcoholic as the booklet had promised: 11.5° Gay Lussac seemed a possible under evaluation, probably a modest understatement, on the part of the excellent, curiously nameless shippers. The only other problem lay in the fact that I was the only member of the bottling line to have taken the whole project sufficiently seriously, having thoroughly washed, rinsed and dried my twenty-four bottles, even having gone to the lengths of baking them all in an oven for forty minutes to sterilize the wretched things. I had also stopped up their necks with wodges of cotton wool to keep out stray spores or bacteria. My partners became unreasonable regarding what they saw as an insufferable proprietorialism upon my part; they refused to assist me in apportioning our individual bottles. I rather think that they muddled them up deliberately *and* removed the cotton wool when I was not looking.

Finally, to demonstrate my sobriety, I conceded the contentious issue, though not without reluctance, and grudgingly allowed myself to be dealt a haphazard assortment.

That night's performance was repeated on a few more occasions, but we decided to stick with 'library' casks: the overflow problem might have been even more considerable with a hogshead, and even we balked at the idea of 'freeing' so many bottles. On the whole the wine was hardly ever *really* convincing, especially for one who had once supped Cheval Blanc 1953. Some of the bottles turned out downright filthy – but those, I decided, had probably never been my bottles in the first place. Still, the wine was incontrovertibly cheap, and the bottles looked comfortable in the racks.

Exotic Encounters

The master guitar player, Julian Bream, is one of the few wine devotees in our locality – that I know of, anyway. The celebrated musician lives in enviable and agreeable seclusion in a rather grand country mansion in the ravishingly pretty countryside to the north of Shaftesbury, ten miles from Mere. We were introduced to each other in 1964 by a mutual friend, the composer Harrison Birtwistle. I was delighted when Harry explained to me that Julian was at about the same stage of over-excitement in the discovery of the marvels of good wine and was exploring the wonders of the *grands châteaux* with a passion to match my own. Soon, Julian and I were capping each other's tales of unearthing amazing bargains almost as fast we uncorked samples of the items in question. We shared other interests too – music (of course), good food, and so on.

I did not acquire the privilege of the care of this new drinking companion's teeth: they were the highly prized domain of an aristocrat of the profession, who plied his expensive manipulations in Harley Street. Nevertheless, one autumn evening I received a telephone call from a plainly distraught Julian. On the point of departure to London Airport, *en route* to give a concert in Düsseldorf, a rather suspect wisdom tooth had inconveniently chosen to flare into agonizing pain. Julian's usual dental attendant was unavailable, dining duchesses at the Connaught.

We quickly agreed to meet at my surgery in half an hour. A little plan was forming in my mind, so I made sure that I arrived first. A store room at the rear of the premises, doing valiant service as an overflow wine cellar, was at that time replete with wine – the harvest of the recent home bottling of a, for once, remarkably pleasing Mâcon *rouge* from the Private Wine Buyers' Society. A sample of this rather tasty beverage was speedily procured and decanted into a tumbler. With dental apparatus prepared for action, instruments at the ready, I thoughtfully placed the 'mouthwash' at the side of the spittoon.

The patient arrived in an unhappy frame of mind, was divested of his coat and coaxed into the dental chair. Diagnosis produced the adamant verdict that the offending molar must be removed with all possible haste. Local anaesthetic administered, we engaged in desultory chat – Julian did not seem to be as cheerfully conversational as usual. At the appropriate moment the offending wisdom tooth was (although I say it myself – admitting to a certain professional pride) deftly extracted. My nod to the miserable patient indicated that he might rinse out his mouth. Julian took a large mouthful of the garnet fluid, and immediately swung his startled eyes in my direction. Staring at me with something akin to horror, with cheeks fully distended as though about to burst, my victim gave me a look of the deepest reproach that I am ever likely to witness. Seconds passed; then the poor fellow swallowed the lot, gulping down the debris of the operation, together with the wine. As soon as he could utter words, he gasped out 'you *utter* bastard!' in bitter tones. We just had time to dispatch the balance of the bottle before my guest drove off into the darkness, towards his awaiting admirers, leaving behind his former property – the tooth that I still retain as a curious souvenir of an unusual occasion.

Another celebrity who resided in the district had achieved a different sort of international fame (or infamy) for a series of exploits that were extremely dubious in nature – but provided enormous amusement to readers of tabloid newspapers. It would scarcely seem possible that half the adventures ascribed to Michael Caborn-Waterfield (affectionately known to his fascinated admirers, eager followers of his erratic and barely credible career, as 'Dandy Kim') could justifiably be laid at his door. Still, he was an ingenious and industrious man, so it was quite possibly the truth.

One of his more notorious contretemps, in the South of France, seemed to hinge on the whereabouts of the immensely valuable jewellery of an American film magnate's wife. Kim later claimed that his subsequent sojourn in a French gaol had been an interesting and educational experience – not least because his privileged post as prison librarian gave ample opportunity for study . . . and for forward planning.

Although well aware of this colourful neighbour's existence, his involvement with the refurbishment of Shaftesbury's Royal Chase

Hotel had quite escaped my attention. News had been abroad for some time that the massive, run-down hotel (at one stage a monastery that must have housed a particularly unworldly, self-abasing holy order) was in course of being revamped, rescued from the dilapidated squalor into which it had been allowed to fall – even the lincrusta, that most durable of decorative materials, was said to have started to disintegrate.

In due course, a 'grand reopening' date was announced, but the ceremony of celebration was not for the likes of us; the 'glitterati' of London's ultra-fashionable social circles (Annabel's was said to have been emptied) were lured to the country for an inaugural Saturday night party, the glamour and excitement of which was the subject of slightly shocked gossip in the hostelries of the district for many weeks after. The only slight catastrophe was said to have been a sudden loss of electricity that had fairly ruined the banquet . . . but the champagne had poured and poured, quite flooding away any possible ennui or tears.

With my brother at home for a few days' break from his latest job (with a pharmaceutical company in Paris), and with a Monday afternoon free, we agreed that it might be amusing to investigate the newly reopened Royal Chase by lunching there. In the event, we were the only customers, the fancy Londoners having decamped back to their habitual West End haunts and Mayfair social whirl. The place was most impressive, strikingly decorated in sub-Moroccan style, perfectly justifying the awed and disbelieving rumours of an extreme sophistication and other-worldly glamour never before seen in our peacefully rustic parts, that had been circulating through our quiet and somewhat introspective society for some weeks. The luncheon had been agreeable, and we were feeling relaxed and contentedly expansive when the neat (expensively, though informally clad) figure of a person of obvious authority in the establishment presented himself at our side, wishing to inquire about our reactions to the meal. Mere pleasantries such as we tried to offer were simply not acceptable, our interlocutor insisted; as the very first (so far, the *only*) paying customers to enter the hotel (the story of Saturday night's débâcle had only just begun its dizzy dissemination around the region, and had not yet reached our ears), only the most stringent and earnestly critical truth would suffice.

Being pushed so hard for ultimate truth, and searching frantically for something helpful in the way of constructive criticism (and with all the weighty authority of a 'silver service' waiter behind me), I suggested that the succulent fillet steak of my *tournedos Rossini* might have been even more the pinnacle of perfection if it had been surmounted by genuine *pâté de foie gras* instead of an irregular cube of tinned Le Parfait. The manager took my kindly intended aspersion with remarkable fortitude and grace, and promised to take steps to eliminate such an appalling solecism immediately. With further encouragement, I diffidently mentioned the only *possible* defect that had occurred to me in the course of the pleasant luncheon; that the wine list was a miserable effort, in fact absolutely hopeless; well, not to mince words, a frightful travesty of the sort of *carte aux vins* to which a restaurant of such obviously high-reaching ambition should aspire. What I may have actually said was that the wine list was a mite . . . uninteresting. After the pause that followed my revelation, Mr Waterfield (for it was indeed he) mildly inquired if I thought that I could produce a better. 'Certainly!' was my imprudent, quick reply.

Kim Waterfield evinced (still does, I am sure – but regrettably I have not run into him for several years) quite the most potent and effective charm of anyone that I have ever met. Perhaps it is not so astonishing as, after all, charm was always his chief stock-in-trade, an attribute he had spent a lifetime perfecting. So, an evening or so later, I took up his invitation to preface a dinner at the hotel with an aperitif at his home, a lovely tile-clad Jacobean manor house a few miles north of Shaftesbury. The sun was sinking as I parked my car in a cobbled stable yard full of flower baskets; as I crunched over the gravel to the entrance porch, my host appeared against the setting sun, approaching across well-tended lawns, accompanied by an aged donkey and a stunningly gorgeous stable-girl.

Inside, the grand reception rooms were sparsely furnished, but what there was had been carefully chosen effectively to form a fabulous stage set. I immediately and, I am sure, correctly surmised that the entire set-up was a *mise en scène*, stage managed to suspend belief. The trio's stroll across the immaculate grass had been simply too perfect not to have been the product of planning and frequent practice. Three immense, gilded baroque thrones which served as the only seating dominated the main *salon*: these and the enormous floor-standing candelabra, each carrying a dozen altar candles, and the elaborately ornamented crystal goblet in which half a pint of high-strength gin and tonic easily swirled (another part of my host's armoury for making unwary visitors utterly at ease?), were all too obviously theatrical not to have been contrived for maximum effect, but it was undeniably impressive to my ingenuous eyes. With no inheritance to squander, absolutely nothing to lose, I decided to relax, sit back and enjoy the night's performance.

Coming up with the goods that I found I had promised some time around the coffee, brandy and cigar stage that night, finding a source of supply for the crisp sort of wine list that I had foolishly claimed to be able to furnish, seemed worryingly problematic – until I suddenly remembered a possible, if pretty unlikely, contact back in Leeds. Two years earlier, I had developed a great longing to examine the evidently fascinating characteristics of a much and reverentially applauded (in the more recherché literature of wine) rarity: a white wine from the Rhône. Apparently very little of this nonpareil (Condrieu by name, and product of the mysterious Viognier grape) was made in *any* year. Just one drop of this fabled elixir was said to make the fortunate consumer swoon with admiration . . . another way of putting it is that this rare white wine was cracked up by self-styled authorities, who seemed fairly sure of their ground, to be an exceptionally pleasant 'drop' with which to slake a thirst.

While still a student in Leeds, I had made the acquaintance of an enterprising wholesale wine and spirits merchant: a crony of, and supplier of wine to, an uncle who was not particularly noted for his abstemiousness, so naturally requiring a wholesale source of supply. This vendor of wine had occasionally sold me a case or two of anything that he considered to be of particular value and/or interest. With all other lines of inquiry failing, I telephoned the man to see if he could help. To my amazement, several months later, this paragon among wine merchants actually managed to lay his hands on some of the elusive Condrieu (Georges Vernay's 1964) and was in a position to let me have a case – or five: that being the minimum quantity that he had had to take. This was bad news, highly embarrassing, because, not surprisingly, the rarity was expensive; in truth, I could scarcely afford a full dozen bottles, certainly not the additional forty-eight. The long-anticipated pleasure derived from the object of my prolonged search was distinctly diminished by the knowledge that the helpful wholesaler must indubitably be in long-term possession of an exotic wine that no one in West Yorkshire was ever likely to have heard of or, if they had, to be able to afford.

This continuing subliminal sense of guilt made the moment all the happier when I suddenly realized that my Leeds connection, so unenviably rich in Condrieu, might be the very person to supply wine to the Royal Chase. My old friend, Ron, appeared to be delighted – so much so that he sped to Dorset forthwith, where he promptly succumbed to the fatal Waterfield charm. The whole enterprise went astonishingly well, particularly considering the awkward logistics of transporting wines from Leeds to Shaftesbury (I would never have the nerve to embark upon such a potentially hazardous responsibility nowadays – not as an amateur; moving wine around the country professionally can be difficult enough). An interesting portent of what the future was to hold was that my selection for the Royal Chase contained a high proportion of Rhône and Loire wines – including Condrieu. A consummate gesture of great thoughtfulness by Waterfield, a cost-free but overwhelmingly effective action utterly typical of his style, afforded me the greatest pleasure: the elegantly designed and superb wine list bore the superscription 'Wines selected by Robin Yapp' – much to the mystification of the *Good Food Guide* the following year, when its entry for the Royal Chase applauded the unusual interest of that establishment's wine list, while plaintively asking 'who on earth is Robin Yapp?' Ron also showed appreciation: when half a dozen bottles of Château Latour 1934 surfaced in a corner of his warehouse, he passed them on to me for a mere 65s each!

Immersion in Bordeaux

My amour with wine had now lasted over ten years, yet I had still never visited the birthplace of the object of my admiration, had not been to France – a dereliction of which I was only too aware. Somehow an increasing family (three children by now) and pressure of work had both contrived to preclude the much longed-for jaunt across the Channel. Only in the spring of 1968 did an expedition become possible. Michael was still tending to the needs of pipeline workers in Algeria, so we arranged to meet at a prearranged hotel in Bordeaux on a certain night in May.

Arriving in Cherbourg at 4.30 p.m. on the date agreed, two major problems, the existence of which I had been increasingly uncomfortably aware for some time, insistently presented themselves. I had never driven my battered Volvo in France, or any other foreign country; rather more worrying was that I spoke no French. Trying to feel bravely undeterred by these considerable disadvantages, I sped off down the Cherbourg Peninsula with all possible dispatch, foolishly imagining that it would be possible to reach Bordeaux at a reasonable hour. So utterly insensible was I to the impossibility of making the distance within the time available that I even took a twenty-minute break in Nantes. It must have been a Saturday because I had read *The Times* as I crossed the Channel, in particular the wine column – always a Saturday feature. The then wine correspondent of *The Times* was the elegant and quasi-aristocratic Colonel Andrew Graham; the burden of his piece that day was the 'ins and outs' of Muscadet. I had learned two completely new facts; that the best Muscadet was made in a peculiarly traditional manner, on the lees, and that there was a subsidiary wine, indigenous to the region, called Gros Plant. My stop in Nantes was at an *estaminet*, expressly to research and to verify this recently discovered information.

A puncture further hindered my headlong canter south. Being virtually allergic to the mechanics of cars, it took ten precious minutes to locate the spare wheel – so cunningly secreted beneath the boot. With much time elapsed, and again mobile, I resumed my hurtling path towards the Médoc. When road signs began to indicate the rapid approach of La Rochelle, I retained sufficient sanity to be prepared to acknowledge defeat. At 9 p.m. I abandoned the trunk road, and limped into La Rochelle, where my deplorable lack of even schoolboy French became ever more disconcerting (I had selected my exploratory glasses of wine in Nantes by dint of pointing at the appropriate bottles). The first hotel at which I called was full (*'absolument complet, Monsieur'*) – if I had correctly understood what they had jabbered at me, or if they had comprehended the nature of my inquiry – the second likewise.

In any normal station, the last train would long since have departed by the time that I made my faltering way into the *buffet de la gare*; only three blue-overalled, seasoned topers still lingered at the zinc-topped bar. In retrospect, I can only imagine that my state of exhaustion was self-evident to the motherly barmaid – because by then I was fast getting beyond the ability to speak: in English or in French. This kindly woman led me upstairs, showed me a sort of bedchamber (M. Michelin had explained that La Rochelle station offered overnight accommodation to benighted travellers – among whose number by then I certainly included myself), the only window of which looked down on to platform 1. I accepted the offered sleeping chamber without demur, with all the non-lingual communicative grace that I could muster, and sank on to the bed – without cleaning my teeth.

The SNCF did not go in for 'last trains' in La Rochelle – *or* for ones that stopped. However, the succession of twenty-minute bursts of unconsciousness (between the violently floor- and bed-shaking passages of express trains) that passed for a short night's sleep alleviated the critical position in which I had been the night before. Settling the account (all of fifteen francs) was a complicated enough affair; ordering breakfast would be clearly impossible – so I had none. After a rapid tour of the town, I resumed the road to Bordeaux, with the inklings of three French expressions instilling themselves in my head: *faites le plein, je voudrais une chambre* and *l'addition, s'il vous plaît*.

I had made an early start – well before 7 a.m. – in part because of a wish to tackle the complications of paying the bill without the benefit of interested bystanders, but also because I was under the impression that Michael would be worried about my whereabouts, and alarmed at my non-arrival in Bordeaux the night before. Eventually, I located the Hotel Sèze, but was met by a puzzling response when I attempted to ascertain my brother's room number. The manager, who *appeared* to wish to be helpful, denied any knowledge of a booking in the name of Yapp. After what seemed an interminable length of time, we jointly thought to turn the page of the hotel's reservation ledger. Somewhere along the line, a mistake had crept in – most probably attributable to my sibling, who was always notoriously disorganized: our rooms had been booked for that very day, *not* the day before. With a most imaginative leap of comprehension (he must have perceived my state of imminent collapse), and with charitable humanity – the like of which I have seldom, if ever, encountered from a Frenchman since – the manager showed me to a vacant room, and smilingly indicated that I was welcome to take a nap.

When I awoke at about midday, the sun was shining. Realizing that Michael would be unlikely to arrive much before early evening, I quickly dressed and started out upon my so long-delayed pilgrimage to the wine châteaux of the Médoc – in a state of high excitement, of course. So very long overdue was this heady encounter with those temples of wine that I could scarcely believe that the places really existed at all. It was extremely difficult to decide between making the briefest pause at as many properties as possible or being more selective and spending a sensible amount of time at a chosen few. Of course I was *not* sensible, and crammed in as many of these, for me, almost fairytale castles as was conceivably possible, taking photograph after photograph in the hope of being able to disentangle the buildings' identities at a later date. The birthplaces of particularly favourite wines were more keenly, and more or less accurately, noted: Cantemerle, Palmer, Ducru Beaucaillou and Beychevelle were positively identified, and the big names, Mouton Rothschild, Lafite and others, gazed upon with reverential awe.

Somewhat reluctantly I drove back to town, dazed by the excitement of the afternoon. As I was attempting to nudge the car into an only just adequate space beside the imposing Grand Théâtre, the door was abruptly pulled open – to my alarm. As chance would have it, my chosen spot was right by the pavement café at which my brother was enjoying a reviving beer after the travails of a journey no less arduous than my own: a sea crossing from Oran to Marseilles, and a lengthy train ride thence to Bordeaux.

My memories of what followed are not always as detailed as I would wish, but certain adventures retain a crystal clarity. The following morning was occupied with the search for a new tyre (the puncture of the night before had been a major burst; at the speed at which I had been travelling I had been amazingly fortunate to avoid a serious accident) – a chore made more complicated by my dearth of French, and the fact that Michael's modest allocation of the language was conveyed in a very strong Algerian accent. With the car safely serviceable again, the châteaux were re-examined in something like tranquillity.

I then decided that the only possible and appropriate souvenir of the voyage must be a case or two of claret. The Maison du Vin, a rather self-important promotional establishment, was singularly unhelpful. Claiming the need to show an absolute impartiality (she said), an unsmiling attendant matron categorically refused to be drawn into imparting anything very useful in the way of advice – simply handing over a full list of every wine firm in Bordeaux. (I was strongly reminded of this Gorgon's inflexibility a few months later, when I asked the French Tourist Board's office in Piccadilly for posters of vineyard scenes with which to decorate my premises. When the publicity material finally arrived, the first depicted the breathtaking Alpine snowfields of a fashionable French ski resort, the next an idyllic autumn Seine-side quay, with a *bateau-mouche* dominated by the Gothic majesty of Nôtre Dame; the third consisted of a sun-drenched, white-sanded beach somewhere on the Côte d'Azur, the foreground attraction being a close-up of a most pleasant young Frenchwoman, whose skimpy bikini barely lent any mystery whatever to her undoubted charms . . . no vines in sight at all.)

So, rather aimlessly, and aggrievedly directionless, we made our way to the Quai des Chartrons where many of the better-known Bordeaux wine houses have their headquarters. Considering the worldwide fame of some of their proprietors, most of the façades of these palaces of wine were rather run down, and not at all inspiring; but pretty soon a sort of self-selection asserted itself. Only one of the buildings had any pretension to elegance and style – indeed, it looked positively handsome and in spankingly well-kept condition and, yes, it was the official residence of an important Bordeaux shipper: above the arched stone doorway the name of Lichine stood elaborately emblazoned.

It so happened that, after Gerald Asher, Alexis Lichine had probably been the most significant influence on my perception of wine; his *Wines of France* had first been published in 1952. It is as attractively written an introduction to wine as I have ever known; but, like so many things that exert a formative influence, Lichine's modest masterwork is elusively difficult to describe: I suspect that it was a combination of an endearing simplicity, an evident intimate knowledge of his subject and the man's sheer exuberant enthusiasm that originally aroused my admiration for the book. Unfortunately for my library, *Wines of France* has always been the 'wine-fuse' that I happily donate to any likely recipient, so that my archives have lacked that first edition for many years. Now subsisting on edition number seven, first published in 1969, I have no doubt that there have been quite a few editions since. Just why this particular treatise has always remained in print over thirty-five years, with nothing that I have ever seen in the way of publicity or publisher's promotion, is a highly satisfactory mystery; perhaps I should form a *Wines of France* enthusiasts' society so that I may meet my fellow devotees.

So we knocked upon the massive wooden door.

The white-painted reception hall was lovely, with a ceiling vaulted as though of monastic origin – with a medieval wooden statue of some saint lending credence to the notion. The greatest blessing to result from our impetuous choice of door was that the French receptionist (for self-preservation, no doubt) immediately summoned a charming English girl to attend to our wishes. Beverly had recently married a Bordelais; that she was a tremendous asset to the company of Lichine was certain. Once she had ascertained my desire to purchase a couple of cases of claret, she pleasantly suggested a visit to the *chai*, the cellars. This turned out not to be an expedition to the vineyards as I initially expected, being well aware that Alexis Lichine owned wine estates in Margaux – the rapidly rising stars of Château Lascombes and Château Prieuré-Lichine, the latter his semi-eponymous home. Our route was merely a few paces' walk through a corridor to the rear of the unusual and attractive vestibule.

As dimly lit ranks of high stacks of wooden wine boxes came into view, we were puzzled to see a couple of bicycles propped against a wall. Before I could voice my curiosity, a blue-overalled workman hurried past us, grabbed one of them and pedalled off into the gloom; the huge warehouses that lie behind the formal architecture of the offices and reception rooms stretch back a good half-mile or more, so bicycles are left at either end to save precious time. The whole, huge cathedral-like space was full – absolutely packed out with wooden-cased claret!

The next hour was spent happily discussing the various possibilities for my intended modest purchase, examining the magical names stencilled on box-ends, but *not* in tasting the precious contents of the bottles inside. Michael suddenly realized that the time had crept to noon, the hour at which all provincial France stops what it is doing, to devote itself to the serious matter of lunch. We immediately suggested making ourselves scarce for the next hour or so, to release our charming guide for her own meal. Promptly agreeing, Beverly suggested that we might care to eat at a small restaurant in the *quartier*, then rejoin her in the *chai* at 2.30 p.m. Upon our gratefully accepting her kind suggestion, she telephoned to reserve a table for us, and scribbled down directions.

When we finally located it, the street looked very dingy – an unlikely location for a recommended restaurant. Only on our third walk past a bead-curtained but otherwise featureless doorway did we dare to put our heads in. The place was very dark, and it was difficult to make things out; as our eyes gradually adjusted to the half-light, we became aware that the room was packed with smartly dressed men and women engaged in earnest conversation while paying equal regard to the contents of their plates. It was just as well that Beverly had booked, as there were only two seats left. Feeling distinctly under-dressed we waited for a menu that somehow failed to materialize. There *was* no menu, we began to understand, as the waitress went on to convey that our choice of entrée lay between a *pâté de foie de volaille* or *saumon fumé*; to make life even more simple, the main course required no deliberation whatsoever: steak was the only thing on offer.

At one end of the restaurant some poor devil of a turnspit was practising for hell at a large raised hearth on which heaped piles of vinewood embers glowed fiercely, bursting into momentary crackling flame as the broiling meat was turned upon the grid. The wine needed as little in the way of a decision as the food: a white wine, a young Chablis, or an equally youthful Beaujolais, Brouilly, were the simple house selection, both bearing the Lichine logo. Rather than embark on yet more French, we indicated our willingness to try a bottle of each – and extremely good they were. As was the food; at once one understood why the place was packed. That luncheon in Bordeaux remains one of the most memorable meals of all. After a while the admirable self-confidence and overall excellence of the restaurant became a little worrying: we had seen no tariff, thus knew no prices; an establishment so clearly supported by an obviously middle-class clientele might well prove to be too expensive for our strictly limited budget. In the end, and to our considerable relief, the bill was really reasonable: ridiculously so, given the indelible memory of quiet, contented pleasure afforded by the whole experience.

Back in the Quai des Chartrons, our new English friend had been doing some organizing; she had arranged to introduce us to the chief oenologist. This important personage was most civil. Luckily, he had a smattering of English, so communication was haltingly possible. When he observed my interest in a highly coloured, framed diploma hanging upon the white tiled wall of his office-cum-laboratory, he told us of the Confrérie des Chevaliers du Tastevin, a brotherhood of burgundy lovers based at Clos de Vougeot, whose certificate of membership it was. A warm description of all the fun that happened at the reunions of the Confrérie, convened several times a year, was as colourful as the manuscript, and caught my imagination. Then, at last, a bottle of wine was produced; as its contents and those of its successor diminished, the oenologist became expansive; if, he said, my brother and I would positively guarantee attendance, he would esteem it an honour to present us to his colleagues of the Confrérie as his protégés, secure our election to the ranks of those blessed burgundian brothers at Clos De Vougeot the following year.

What with one thing and another, we walked away from the Maison Lichine in an exhausted state of happy euphoria. In my hand, I clutched a green piece of paper, an official Lichine bill of transaction, a document carefully and neatly enumerating the sixty-two cases of wine that I had apparently insisted upon ordering during the course of the afternoon: all for shipment to Mere, via Shoreham, within very few days.

On the morrow, and under the circumstances, it seemed rather a good idea to quit Bordeaux, to explore the countryside, and to do our best to recover our composure. Though not before one last wine-dedicated excursion, which was to pay respects to Château Cheval Blanc. An introduction to a highly reputed *courtier* (wine trade middle-man) in Libourne had been arranged by an accommodating London shipper. The *courtier* had been charged with the task of leading us to the cradle of my revelatory Cheval Blanc 1953. It all went very badly wrong. The man was in an evil temper, his guaranteed excellent command of English had totally gone on strike, he plainly did not like us or want anything to do with us: that we were simply a nuisance was made absolutely clear. Only an obligation to our mutual London contact had made him turn up at our hotel in Saint Emilion at all; his intention of conducting the promised tour at record speed was all too evident.

Only the building, the château itself, did not disappoint. Our surly guide muttered something inaudible to an equally morose *maître de chai*, who promptly extinguished the minimal semblance of attentiveness that his unpromising features had hitherto displayed. No, to taste the young wine would *not* be possible; the wine had just been racked and, anyway, was far too precious for the likes of us. Any residual confidence we felt rapidly ebbed as Michael tried, at my behest, to explain my 'road to Damascus conversion' story to the ungracious guardian of the fountainhead (I felt that the fluency of the telling of this remarkable history was a *trifle* undermined by my brother's thickly Algerian-accented French). The wine maker then delivered his *coup de grâce* with flat finality: he really was not interested in such nonsense – he had not been working at Cheval Blanc at that period, did not know the vintage in question, neither did he care. My romantic passion for all matters vinous took quite a dent that afternoon . . . but only temporarily.

The following days were as happily fulfilling as Cheval Blanc had been crushing. The picturesque villages of the Dordogne, Lot and Tarn, the rivers themselves, swimming in an invigoratingly chilly

Célé (when an elderly black-clad woman took time off from pounding her laundry with boulders at the river's edge to help push-start the car, which had a flat battery), riverside picnics with fresh new season's asparagus cooked to perfection in a billycan, white wine cooling among riverbed pebbles – all served to present a grateful first view of provincial pastoral France that exceeded even *my* expectations and most earnest imaginings.

Our preoccupation with this wonderful voyage of confirmation and discovery had cut us off from the world at large. We did not pick up a newspaper; television sets in hotels were far less common in 1968 than they are today, and our perennial problem in communicating with the natives precluded our being privy to the state of affairs in places other than this peacefully idyllic corner of France. Only when we started north did minor problems start to arise. When we crossed the Loire, our efforts to telephone the famous then three-star Michelin restaurant of M. Barrier in Tours met inexplicable difficulties: something seemed to be badly awry with the French telephone system (never considered to be anything other than laughably inefficient, even on its better days). Further north, in Normandy, an increasingly severe dearth of petrol became apparent, persistent gesturing being needed to abstract a mere few litres from curiously reluctant garage owners.

The car ferry quays at Cherbourg were in an astonishing state of disarray; hundreds of distraught English tourists were panicking on the quayside with an abandon that was positively Gallic in its noisy lack of self-consciousness. While we had been contentedly pottering through the quiet by-ways of the Dordogne, France had been in the grips of urban riot and revolution (a demonstrator had been killed in Bordeaux on the day of our departure to the country); the universities were in turmoil, all public services disrupted, and now every exit port was blocked by strike action – every one but Cherbourg. Somehow, little by little, we were able to pick our way through the unhappy milling throng, and get the car aboard the awaiting ferry – our place had been booked prior to the holiday and reservations were being honoured, despite the general mayhem. Finally, and much against what appeared possible at first glance, the ship's crew somehow contrived to find room aboard for every British vehicle and passenger and squeezed into the confines of the boat all the desperate refugees from already blockaded Le Havre; no one was left to languish upon the quay when the last ferry to leave France for nearly a month quietly slipped her moorings to start the voyage home.

Public Launch

Sixty-two cases of wine, now imminently due to arrive from Bordeaux, were going to take a great deal of explaining; were probably totally inexplicable so far as a distinctly unsympathetic bank manager was likely to be concerned. Relations with the Gillingham bank were still not what might be described as cordial. The then manager, successor to the worthy man whom I had originally importuned for fiscal support at the debut of my practice, always succeeded in emanating a slight air of disapproval regarding the fact that a relatively high proportion of the individually modest financial transactions that invariably (and *so* mysteriously) accumulated into recurrent, bright red fever spots in my quarterly statements tended to relate to the urgent monetary appeasement of various wine suppliers who had kindly forwarded me small shipments of their (sometimes) excellent wares on helpful credit terms. Perhaps the counterfoils of my used cheque books *were* rather more punctuated with the names of celebrated wine merchants than were those of others of the bank's no doubt estimable clientele. In any event, the man's conspicuous lack of sympathy with, and stiff-necked incomprehension of, the mild interests and simple pleasures of a hard-working country dentist always made my occasional visits to the bank (usually at his request) rather uncomfortable affairs. Only the beautiful and inescapable truth that mine was the only dental practice in the town and that I, in my capacity as the only dentist, had the dubious biannual privilege of tending the manager's teeth (and those of his family, *and* those of the majority of his staff) allowed me to preserve anything in the way of carefree insouciance upon the occasion of these tediously boring financial chats.

A possible plea for sympathy, a bid for mitigation, regarding the mischief caused by my marvellous moment of exhilaration in Bordeaux might have been along the lines of: what sane wine lover could conceivably have passed up the unexpected opportunity of giving home to, of cellaring, umpteen examples of the product of some of the most highly regarded vineyards of the Médoc in the fast becoming legendary vintage of 1961? Certainly not I. What a dizzy choice: Lascombes and Prieuré-Lichine, of course – common politeness to our amiable hosts on the Quai des Chartrons demanded a positive interest in those estates, so why not a case of each in the reasonably well-applauded year of 1966 at the same time? Yes, definitely a good idea; and although 1964 did not receive adulation at its inception, that could well have been an underestimation on the part of fallible journalists, and the most evident virtue had to be the cheapness of the vintage; anyway, to have the same wines, Prieuré and Lascombes, in three different vintages would always allow interesting comparisons to be made in years to come – so add them to the list. And so on . . . Cantemerle, Ducru Beaucaillou, Beychevelle, Lynch Bages, all obvious candidates; Gaffelières Naudes too – all of the fabulous year of 1961, and all at a bargain rate of between 25s and £2. The decision to invest in Château Mouton Rothschild took fractionally more deliberation: after all, £3 5s 4½d a bottle by the time that it had been shipped and the duty paid (then £3 14s a dozen, I believe) was a major disbursement of the bank's resources. Inevitably, an immutable law of nature (as probably first propounded by Einstein himself) subsequently dictated that the only breakage to be found among the sixty-two cases, within the ranks of 744 bottles, on the shipment's arrival at Hinckes Mill House, the sole casualty, was that of one of the twenty-four bottles of Château Mouton Rothschild 1961.

No, it seemed to me that, for once, I had displayed astoundingly sound judgement in ordering those vinous gems – and, of course, I have gleefully hugged myself in joyous satisfaction over the intervening years, as I have watched the sale-room value of those fifteen assorted 1961 clarets soar inexorably higher, now well inaccessible to my reach. I bought the wines to drink and, in due course, fully intend to do just that; only three bottles have so far been broached, and those only in recent months: the excellent news is that Lascombes, Lynch Bages and Pichon Longueville Lalande are coming along a treat, particularly the Lascombes. The twenty-three bottles of Mouton remain untouched – for the moment at least: perhaps I should take a thoughtful look at the contents of one of their number before too long.

It was the Chablis that seemed to be rather more of a curious choice. A most excellent example of the genre, I had concluded in the course of that simple but memorable luncheon in Bordeaux: as coincidence would have it, the same Chablis was the wine so liberally poured by the genial oenologist during that hazily remembered afternoon. It appeared that somewhere along the line I had become so enamoured of it that I had insisted on registering a request for twenty cases of the stuff . . . together with fifteen cases of Brouilly.

Merely taken from a quality: price ratio viewpoint, my judgement (or lack of it) eventually proved to have been impeccable: both wines were truly delicious. The Beaujolais, Brouilly 1966, cost £4 6s 6d a case FOB – with transport cost and customs duty included, 12s 7½d a bottle delivered to Mere; the Chablis, also 1966 and from the vineyard of a M. Boudin, totalled out at 13s 2d . . . *and* both wines were estate-bottled!

Certain pertinent aspects of estate-bottling, as perpetrated by the company of Lichine, were to present me, for a while at any rate, with niggling worries and uneasy doubts. I now admire the Lichine system as the product of an inspirational and totally justified self-confidence but, for a time, the ethical and moral issues involved occasioned some disquiet. A short time previously, a bright, lateral-thinking employee had devised a most ingenious scheme where the firm had fitted out an ultra-efficient bottling plant on the back of a small truck, thus creating a highly mobile bottling line, which was then dispatched to pursue a seemingly erratic zig-zag course through the smallholdings of Chablis, Beaujolais, Burgundy and so on, bottling merrily as it went.

Undoubtedly, the wines thus bottled *had* been *mis en bouteille* at the property of origin, be it a vineyard of half an acre only: all seemingly so simple . . . but breathtakingly brilliant as an original concept. The only possible drawback of this fascinating undertaking lay in any unevenness of quality which might result from the selection, in many cases, of tiny volumes of wine. As Georges Duboeuf has subsequently (and extremely successfully) demonstrated in the Beaujolais, with flair, self-confidence and dedication available, the whole complicated business is eminently viable – the genius lies in the careful initial choice of which small grower to support and, no doubt, in his continuing education. A pioneer in a potential minefield of viticulture and vinification, the House of Lichine succeeded to marvellous perfection in its cheeky estate-bottling ploy: the quality of Lichine's 'estate-bottled' wines was always impeccable.

Which admirable fact did not really aid my present predicament. My own enthusiasm for the wines, no matter how perfect they might be, was scarcely likely to impress or sway the opinions of a deeply sceptical bank manager, a philistine who evinced every appearance of considering even a single bottle of wine to be shamefully decadent, a luxury quite alien to the peaceful dairylands of North Dorset . . . a latent Luddite bottle-breaker, he – if ever I saw one! A few friends did their utmost to support and succour me at this difficult time – taking the odd case off my replete hands, but their annual rate of wine absorption was of the miserable volume that had consistently helped to keep Britain at the bottom of all the statistical tables of world wine consumption, so their well-intended efforts did not even begin to lick my wine puddle dry. The problem was fast becoming an emergency.

As any vestigial credibility that I had ever enjoyed with the bank rapidly ebbed away, the necessity of finding a definitive solution to the quandary became imperative: I resolved to take advertising space in a national newspaper. Having ascertained the cost of a quarter-inch single column in the *Sunday Times* and *Observer*, I booked those minimal spaces for the next edition of both. The first announcement of the availability of wine from Yapp was simplicity itself: Chablis 1966 from the estate of M. Boudin and bottled thereon (but paucity of lines regrettably precluded any circumstantial explanation of the intricacies of the Lichine estate-bottling system) at 19s 6d a bottle, £11 14s by the dozen. At the last moment, as I penned this simple legend, a thought passed through my mind concerning some guilt-instilling Condrieu that must perforce be languishing yet in Leeds – the Royal Chase wine list had only accounted for three bottles, one of which Kim Waterfield had dispensed to Ron and me at dinner one night eighteen months before, in a typical gesture of generous hospitality – so that I estimated that the chances of forty-five bottles remaining a drug on the Leeds wine market were pretty well certain. In foolishly cavalier fashion, I neglected to verify that my guess as to the Condrieu stock situation in West Yorkshire was indeed correct; I just added the exotic rarity to the contents of the advertisement: Condrieu 1964, Georges Vernay, 32s 6d a bottle, £19 10s a case – a dizzy sum.

Those initial advertisements actually engendered orders: five to be precise. One was for a case of Chablis (discerning people) but, to my utter amazement, three were for Vernay's (and Ron's) Condrieu *by the case* (one of the supplicants being Mr Dennis Wheatley, celebrated author of such lurid romances of the occult and supernatural as *To the Devil a Daughter* and *The Devil Rides Out*, but evidently a man of the utmost refinement when it came to wine), and the last was from a troublemaker who wanted six bottles of each. A frantic telephone call to Ron in Leeds confirmed my earlier cynicism about his fellow citizens' appreciation of fine wine; there were indeed forty-five bottles of M. Vernay's delicious elixir very much available, gladly at my disposal.

The same telephone conversation imparted essential information about the physical distribution of wine. Ron volunteered to wing the complete cases of Condrieu to my new-found clients – Mr Wheatley and his fellow founders of the Yapp supporters' club, and six bottles to me with a make-weight half-dozen of something cheap and cheerful as a token of thanks for this eventual deliverance (I suspect that he splurged the other three on a wild bacchanal of personal celebration – probably incorporating the incomparable liquid treasure in some dangerously noxious wine cup). Possibly more valuable than anything else that my blunt northern acquaintance gave me was excellent advice about nationwide carriers and their tricky little ways: distributing their wares was, and remains, the major and perennial problem besetting all would-be mail order merchants.

Reasonably successful then, that first bid for international recognition as a wine merchant (and I suppose that it marked my debut in the trade), but it still left me the rueful possessor of an embarrassing volume of absolutely splendid Chablis surplus to personal requirements. Yet the initial vestiges of an idea had also been derived from the novel experiment; it would seem that out there, in the great wide world, existed a potential market for good, if relatively little-known, wines coming from vineyards other than those of Burgundy or the Médoc. It might *perhaps* be feasible to specialize in particular wines . . . such as the highly interesting, truly estimable, but thoroughly neglected wines of the Loire and Rhône.

While the amalgamation of one wine company with another, and the absorption of smaller individual firms by larger enterprises –

most notably the large brewery conglomerates – had produced the marvellous windfall wine bargains of the early and middle 1960s, precisely the same phenomenon had served to iron out that interesting individuality that had always been the justification, the *raison d'être* of the old-fashioned, traditional family businesses which in some instances had adorned the trade for centuries. As stony-faced accountants began to gain ascendancy in the running of affairs, choice necessarily became more limited. Hard-hearted computers most definitely frowned upon idiosyncratic dealings in low-volume products, autocratically declaring the non-viability (in ledger terms) of any commerce in wines of unheard-of provenance . . . the barbarians had arrived. Throughout my formative wine-learning and drinking years, I had taken more than passing glances over my shoulder at the Rhône and Loire and, in the process, had subliminally developed a pronounced appreciation of the virtue, honesty, and plain good value of the products of those regions. Obviously Gerald Asher had had a similar idea, had believed in the same tenets as I was now beginning to formulate; but could it not have been the dilution of the principle by the addition of, or sticking to, the traditional British wine merchant's wares, the punitively costly holding of stocks of claret and burgundy, that had played a part in his ultimate regrettable lack of success? An interesting thought . . .

On the Monday following the second appearance of the advertisements (which by then were offering Chablis and Brouilly, stocks of Condrieu having definitely been exhausted and its promotion indefinitely suspended) I was mildly surprised to see a car at the side of the lane that led to Hinckes Mill House, upon my return home from morning surgery. The road system around the house was a minor maze of virtual trackways, leading nowhere in particular, and fairly inaccessible to anyone not determined to penetrate their intricacies, so the presence of a strange vehicle was noteworthy in itself. The car's occupant hopped smartly out as I approached the house, and vigorously hailed me. His message was straightforward, and commendably brief; the West Country representative of a well-known London wine company, he had received a telephone call the previous evening from his managing director, instructing him to find me and to commence negotiations directly. Impressed by the poor man's evident aptitude for private detection work (Hinckes Mill House was peculiarly difficult to locate) and by his dedicated patience and praiseworthy devotion to duty in having awaited my return over several boring hours, I swiftly rewarded his vigilance with a large glass of cool, refreshing . . . Chablis.

The two appearances of my advertisements had attracted the attention of the wine rep's boss. For some momentarily unexplained purpose of his own, the great man urgently wished the favour of an interview: when would I be available for a meeting at his London cellars? The following Tuesday, as it happened.

The idea of investigating a real, live, *authentic* professional London cellar was enormously appealing; though quite what I thought I would see is difficult to explain. As I travelled by train to Waterloo Station, towards this mysterious rendezvous with a totally unknown host, my curiosity and stirrings of excitement were aroused and fuelled by useless speculation as to the purpose of the meeting. The company's cellars and at least some of its offices were housed in two large arches in Tooley Street, tunnelled beneath the approach tracks of London Bridge Station, just a few hundred yards along the street from the entrance to Guy's Hospital. Definitely on the early side for the 11.30 a.m. appointment, I took the opportunity to stroll over London Bridge (the one that now straddles a brackish lake in Texas, at some desert holiday resort – having been transported there at breathtaking expense for reconstruction under an alien sun, stone by numbered stone); the district was new to me, so it was temporarily calming to pick out the grey and white crenellation of Southwark Cathedral's tower, to wince at the tidal wave of fish aroma wafting from Billingsgate Market and to admire a splendid vista of the Thames, framed by the neo-Gothic magnificence of Tower Bridge. The subterranean archways beneath London Bridge Station have given home to wine shippers for many years; a faint smell of wine hung in the air, replacing that of fish, as I ambled down Tooley Street – beginning, by this stage, to feel decidedly nervous.

At my first knock upon the small postern gate let into one of the archway entrance's two large wooden doors, I was greeted by a cellarman, who indicated the direction of the director's cellar office (the main showplace reception office, and the man's more usual habitat, being in Bond Street). I passed through extensive, whitewashed, vaulted cellars which were roomy and housed countless cardboard cartons, all presumably replete with bottles of delicious wine. Initial identification and greetings over, the managing director conducted me to a tasting room behind his office. The scenario of my visit had, it dawned upon me, been extremely carefully arranged with a sense of theatricality that would have stood comparison with any of Kim Waterfield's most contrived endeavours in the field of trying to impress a simple country dentist with visions of glamour and extraordinary sophistication. A white-overalled head cellarman was in the final throes of arranging the last bottles of a sample of each of the firm's range of more than two hundred wines upon a shelf that ran around three sides of the not tiny room.

My host, a traditional old-school semi-patrician of distinguished and dignified appearance, Brigade of Guards tie immaculately knotted, possibly sixty years of age, was impressive enough, almost awesome, in his own right; the serried ranks of brightly gleaming, colourfully labelled bottles made an extremely jolly sight; the head cellarman might well have done a stint at RADA, so impeccable was his assumption of an evidently demanded role of deferentially attentive batman, a sort of low-key master of ceremonies, at the rapidly approaching performance. Then this solemn attendant produced a useful-looking corkscrew, as the managing director quietly conveyed to my incredulous ears that, if I were so minded and were to utter words of assent or of command, the bearer of the apparatus would promptly employ it to withdraw the cork from each and every bottle that constituted the brave display.

As I had *never* been anywhere near any sort of professional tasting, the situation seemed . . . problematic. What was the usual form on these occasions? Did one spit out (I could not remember ever spitting out good wine, or envisage such *lèse-majesté*)? If so, then where? (Oh, presumably the sawdust-filled buckets which the cellarman now placed at regular intervals along the floor.) What in the world were these proffered samples, anyway? Some appeared to be black-Gothic-scripted German wines – something about which I knew nothing whatsoever. The straw that a rural person carries in his hair on visits to the city began to prickle my scalp even more uncomfortably, but I prudently said nothing; just thought as fast as I was able. It seemed a reasonable enough proposition to examine the bottles' labels, to scrutinize the legends on them, and I tentatively began to do so. Some God-given residual common sense imparted, despite my confusion, the wisdom of restricting tasting to a maximum of, say, a dozen wines. With the greatest difficulty, I managed to suppress the 'child let loose in a toy shop' syndrome, and slowly began to make a selection.

Miraculously, another penny dropped; I allowed my innate but surfacing interest in Loire and Rhône to help dictate my choice. It so happened that the company held the agency for a particularly well-known *négociant* house based at Ampuis, in the Northern Rhône; what with the Vidal-Fleury wines, and a handful of straightforward Loires, I was able to come up with a dozen wines with which I might expect to be reasonably and respectably conversant, and about which I might just possibly tender a guardedly non-committal comment. The whole business was so highly improbable and so extraordinarily strange that there was no pleasure in it at the time (more like unbridled fear!), but I think that I realized, even then, the amusement to which the whole incident might eventually give rise. Any detailed memories of that tasting are long gone (if the tension of the occasion did not obliterate them as the charade unfolded – which is likely), but the memory of my first sighting of the distinctive labels of the firm of Vidal-Fleury, maker of the examples of Côte Rôtie, Châteauneuf-du-Pape and Hermitage that I sampled in Tooley Street that day remained with me, and was to become something of a catalyst in days to come.

The ordeal over, luncheon was suggested, and the hospitality accepted. Now, as we walked along Tooley Street towards Borough High Street, passing the premises of hop merchants, and a famous Elizabethan pub, the wooden-galleried George, my new acquaintance (now a far less awesome 'Ralph') began to put forward his intended scheme: the whole reason for this dramatic whirlwind courtship. The finer points were explained as we waited for steak, kidney and oyster pudding in the convivial atmosphere of a sawdust-scattered, clever recreation of a late seventeenth-century London ale house called the Boot and Flogger – John Davy's pilot venture in what has now become a successful chain of such establishments. Ralph's suggestion was exceedingly simple and really most attractive: that I should continue with my modest advertising campaign . . .

at his company's expense . . . provided that two-thirds of any wines thus marketed would be taken from his cellars.

I was still attempting to detect any flaws or pitfalls in this admirably terse scheme when we re-entered the cellars by the postern gate. All reservations disappeared, my legs were cut away from under me, my seduction complete, when my new friend and potential benefactor wandered over to a rack of grimy cobwebbed bottles, and pulled out a black whitewash-dabbed veteran for immediate decanting into carafe, and thence into us. Possible lingering apprehensions and any inhibitions concerning the wisdom of the proposition evaporated in a trice as I contemplated first one, then another, brimming glassful of legendary Taylor's '27.

The arrangement worked quite well, to our mutual satisfaction, for quite some time. The advertisements appeared regularly, carrying the details of, always, the Chablis (but now part of a second shipment from Bordeaux), several other Lichine estate-bottled offerings – this time from the Loire – and various excellent wines from the cellars of a reputable London merchant, Vidal-Fleury's Châteauneuf-du-Pape, Hermitage and Côte Rôtie looming large upon the list.

As the weeks went by, the idea of specializing in the wines of the Loire and Rhône took firmer hold and shape, simultaneously with a wish to publish a list of wines for sending to an embryonic mailing list of apparently interested parties. I realized that a simple (though it proved highly effective) way to build up a core of decent wines, good examples of both my favoured viticultural regions, would be to study the catalogues of *all* the London wholesale shippers, culling from them the very best wines – acting as a sort of wine clearing house; so that is what I did. Establishing business relations with firms such as Reynier, Loeb, Atkinson Baldwin, Hellmers and others was relatively straightforward; getting these people to take me seriously was quite another matter.

Aug. Hellmers and Sons Limited specialized in fine German wine, but also represented the famous Rhône *négociant* house of Chapoutier which, like Paul Jaboulet Aîné (Loeb held *that* agency), was firmly based in the very shadow of the hill of Hermitage, at Tain l'Hermitage on the east bank of the Rhône. Hellmers had their offices in the forecourt of London Bridge Station, their cellars being half a mile away, somewhere beneath the railway lines.

My imagination had been captured by a glowing account in an article by the late Denzil Batchelor – sports journalist and wine-loving bon viveur – in which he colourfully described an important luncheon, a celebrated affair, held annually at their offices by Hellmers. The idea of the combination of a monster tasting, where sixty or more wines (any inhibitions once held as to how many wines could be tasted at one sitting were fast disappearing; though twenty to twenty-five now seem to be as many wines as one should sensibly confront at any one time) were available for assessment, and a plain but well-prepared meal to which the fortunate guests were admonished to bear one or two of whichever of the tasting wines happened to have taken their fancy, conjured up an extraordinary picture of enviable privilege, particularly as depicted by Batchelor's felicitous prose.

The managing director then presiding over these feasts was a marvellous man called Ronnie Scott, a twinklingly charming, slightly roguish person whose kindness was legendary and whose fund of not always funny stories was *fairly* inexhaustible (just occasionally a story would have caused him so much amusement that its retelling became repetitive: I grew to nurse a keen desire *never* to hear the saga about the 'King Edwards' again). Ronnie had spent a lifetime in the wine trade, and ran Hellmers in autocratic and idiosyncratic fashion. His only annoying trait was his unwillingness to take my emerging ambitions seriously; but he readily gave me a standing invitation to lunch with him in his office. The joys of the meal might be debatable – the fairly dire grub knocked up by a morose charwoman devoid of culinary inspiration somewhat taking the edge off the pleasure afforded by the generously offered wines – but I exploited the privilege with what may well have been cheeky over-frequency, and was fast becoming fond of my mildly garrulous host.

However, Ronnie continued to laugh his head off at what he had firmly decided were wild pretensions to being a wine merchant, totally refusing to believe that a mere dentist could stand the hurly-burly of the commercial wine world. He was perfectly prepared to supply me with M. Chapoutier's excellent wines on generously favourable terms, insisted upon my attendance at the famous annual tasting luncheon, but still snorted with uncontrollable mirth if he detected any signs of my taking myself a little too seriously on the matter of wine. Ronnie's death ten years ago was a sad loss to his many friends, and he is greatly missed; I cannot help nursing a sneaking regret that he cannot see that, contrary to all his amused expectation, I am still managing to hang on to the fringes of the trade.

Other London shippers were just as generous, and humoured my initial efforts with kindness and a great deal of practical assistance. They helped me to put together a reasonably creditable first list, which included several items peripheral to my specialities. William and Humbert's Dos Cortados, a palo cortado sherry is an especially pleasing wine which I then described as 'rare and exquisite', which indeed it is. A palo cortado falls somewhere between amontillado and oloroso in style, having an intensely rich but subtle bouquet, and a surprisingly dry, complex flavour that quite belies the powerful concentration of aroma.

It is not easy to give a totally satisfactory account of why my new wine business became known as Yapp Brothers. My only brother lived and worked mostly abroad; while happy enough to quaff his share of any decent bottle, he lacked my slightly obsessive devotion to wine. A ten-year age difference seemed to have brought us to a closer friendship than is sometimes the case between less widely separated siblings, so it was, I think, affection that brought about the company title – coupled, perhaps, with a thought that the name had an old-fashioned ring to it which might serve to instil useful confidence in possible customers. Although Michael certainly wished me well, taking an amused fraternal interest in the progress of my 'baby', he had no further involvement in the business's affairs.

At the time that I was assembling the first catalogue, I gave him one commission; I was anxious to use two appreciative descriptions of Dos Cortados – one written by Julian Jeffs for a Condé Nast magazine in 1966, extolling the merits of the wine. The second, no less enthusiastic, piece had appeared in another Condé Nast organ, *House and Garden*, in April 1969, and came from the inimitable pen of Edmund Penning-Rowsell – great claret guru, and a hero of mine by virtue of his marvellous writing about that wine in *Country Life*, the *Financial Times* and the definitive treatise on the subject, his book *Bordeaux*.

As Michael was on the point of returning to Paris, he realized that matters were in danger of getting out of hand, as he saw me struggling with the preparation of the list. He offered to help if and where possible; gratefully, I suggested that he write on my behalf to the two writers, to elicit their permission to reprint the relevant portions of their articles. When my brother reappeared in England four months later, the list had been printed and distributed to the thirty-seven eager souls who clearly burned to possess a copy. As I uncorked a bottle of sparkling wine, I casually asked to see the authors' replies. 'Oh', said my unperturbed brother, 'I *knew* that there was *something* that you had asked me to do . . .' Feeling fervently thankful that Messrs Jeffs and Penning-Rowsell had not yet been enrolled in the happy band of Yapp brochure recipients, I swiftly wrote my plea to plagiarize their pieces, carefully concealing the fact that any forthcoming permission had already been pre-empted several months earlier. Both graciously granted their consent – though Edmund Penning-Rowsell appended the suggestion that a £5 reimbursement might not come amiss.

In an effort to have something potable at the bottom end of the price range, I added a brace of Algerian wines to the inside back cover of the list; the mildly alcoholic liquid in question represented yet another liaison with Leeds: the wine came via Ron. With vivid memories of my several expeditions (only the first was professional) through Algeria, I dubbed the red 'Grande Kabylie' (swearing, in print, that it was 'a robust and full-flavoured red wine' – no one quarrelled with the last adjective or, in the event, with the other two), named for a region of craggy mountains and blue-tattooed women (*and* falling rocks: a large one narrowly missed our car); the 'pleasant dry white' I called 'Zelfaner', in honour of the hot springs in the Sahara where I had celebrated my twenty-seventh birthday. The labels were printed in Gillingham, and I stuck them on the bottles in the evening, only mistaking the correct colour as the night wore on. At 9s 6d a bottle the wine was quite a snip, though I must confess that they were not the bottles upon which I *often* felt obliged to exercise quality control. After eighteen months or so, I began to sense that the nature of the wines had, in some way, altered: not more, or less, acceptable; simply different. Upon my earnest inquiries, Ron reluctantly admitted that the source of the supposed Algerians had changed several times since their arrival on the scene, Austria being current holder of the baton. I was fully prepared to agree that both countries began with an 'A', but that was when Grande Kabylie and Zelfaner quietly exited from the list.

Business could not have been described as remotely brisk; the profits on sales of five cases a week were never going to supplant a dental income – not that that was my intention, but I strongly and seriously felt the need to create a genuinely viable business, *not* a dilettante pastime that might just conceivably cover the cost of my own wine consumption. It was high time to address my attention to the gentle art of publicity, the moment to make amiable contact with the wine writers . . . and who better to start with than the revered Mr Penning-Rowsell?

It took half an hour's reflection to dredge up a possible plan of campaign. The letter to my idol expressed my admiration for him in, quite possibly, over-fulsome terms, and went on to present an attempt at a synopsis and a rather over-optimistic projection of my scheme to specialize in the wines of Rhône and Loire. This carefully constructed missive concluded upon something like these lines: 'If you are minded to make the fatiguing train journey from London in order to dine and to spend the night with us, would you mind awfully if a fellow admirer of yours, a chap called Julian Bream, comes to dinner too, which, upon reflection, would furnish a most propitious pretext to decant one of my last bottles of Château Cheval Blanc 1953.' As any remotely civilized person would, Edmund Penning-Rowsell arrived on virtually the very next train.

The encounter was a happy one; we all got on extremely well, Julian behaved himself *reasonably* well, the Cheval Blanc was fantastic, and Edmund tried to refund the £5, embarrassed that he had ever thought of asking for a fee. As I waved him farewell at Gillingham Station, he called out something about a return match in the not too distant future.

The next victim that I lured down to Hinckes Mill House was my informant on the minutiae of Muscadet as I first passed over the Channel to France. Andrew Graham's visit could not be described as a happy affair; it was absolutely disastrous. The time of arrival that he had given me was, it turned out, wrong: no London train had arrived, or would arrive, within an hour of the stated time. So, somewhat exhausted after a busy surgery, I headed back to Mere. Hardly had I divested myself of my jacket, when the telephone rang.

An extremely unhappy, not to say near-hysterical, Mr Graham had, it appeared, completely misread the railway timetable; my anticipated guest had somehow succeeded in finding a completely unheard-of (to us locals) waiting room at the station and had thus eluded my comprehensive search. This call was, perforce, made from a telephone kiosk in the High Street – while, as I had just learned, the station now boasted an inconspicuous waiting room, as yet it lacked a telephone.

I imagine that I broke the North Dorset Rugby Club's All-Comers' Challenge in my return-journey time between Mere and Gillingham to encounter the honoured guest: a white-faced, non-communicative, silently furious Andrew Graham. As we swung through the High Street, he broke his stony silence to inquire, abruptly, if I had an adequate supply of soda siphons at the house. Realizing that all was less than well, and rather than admitting to a further dereliction, I simply halted at the door of an off-licence and leapt out to purchase several siphons.

At Hinckes Mill House, Mr Graham retreated silently to the guest room, armed with a tumbler that contained an octuple measure of whisky and one of the soda siphons . . . and would *not* come out. Downstairs on the hall sideboard an array of fifteen to twenty bottles, the *crème de la crème* of my modest range, awaited the visitor's attention. Dinner guests (Julian among their number) arrived, but still the dratted man would not descend. Yet *further* abject apologies and all imaginable blandishments (whispered through the bedroom door) eventually bore fruit. Reluctantly, and very, very slowly, Andrew deigned to unlock the door and quietly descend – looking really rather fetching, in a white angora pullover and the daintiest pair of black patent leather, silver-buckled slippers I had ever seen.

He would take no interest whatsoever in the well-aligned row of bottles, did not wish to taste them, stalked unswervingly past them, would *not* be made to pause; growling impatiently for another quarter pint of Bell's, he proceeded to the conservatory where the discontent upon his brow managed to reduce the other guests to monosyllabic mutterings. Far more gradually than I would have wished, the whisky worked its potent magic; the wine correspondent of *The Times* began to calm down, visibly to relax, actually show vestiges of a reputed charm. He perked up considerably with assistance from the champagne (an oldish vintage of Bollinger) and began to converse with his neighbours at table. Another sacrificial decanter of Cheval Blanc 1953 evaporated . . . but he did not appear to notice.

At the earliest stage of negotiations concerning his expedition into the country, Mr Graham had laid particular stress upon an unusual (but clearly important – more so than even the soda siphons) condition: a firm guarantee had been required, positively insisted upon, that he would be afforded facilities to make tea in his room; a promise to that effect had been made. Quite clearly, all possible finesse ought to be exercised in the fulfilment of such a significant desire. An unassailably perfect porcelain tea cup and saucer were procured, gingerly removed from the glazed protection of a secretaire-bookcase, the baby contributed a silver christening spoon, an elegant eighteenth-century Sheffield plate tea caddy was lightly and lovingly caressed into gleamingly reflective glory, and a silver Georgian *bombé* sugar basin borrowed from my brother; all this exquisite assemblage was then arranged with careful and caring precision upon a handsome galleried Sheffield plate tray.

At the interminable evening's end, adieux were made between all the protagonists, with an underlying feeling of hope that all had not been quite so terrible after all; with the beneficent passage of time it might, eventually, be possible to construe the entertainment as *almost* a success. When I sought the distinguished visitor at the requested hour of 8 a.m., the fury of his mien quite eclipsed that of the previous evening; the man would not communicate in any way – other than by an alarmingly discernible twitching in the region of his left temple; any sort of breakfast was declined in tersest terms; the black valise was thrust forward for immediate consignment to the back seat of the car. The five-mile drive to Gillingham was totally unrelieved by attempts at conversation; Mr Graham boarded the 9 a.m. train to Waterloo in tight-lipped, obdurate silence.

Only when I retrieved the tea ceremony paraphernalia from the spare room later in the day did the reason for my guest's annoyance (an understatement, to put it mildly) become clear; the Sheffield plate tray, with its various pretty bibelots, made a strikingly handsome sight . . . but I had neglected to charge the tea caddy with tea . . . That Mr Graham was an old and seasoned campaigner was evident: he had been able to overcome adversity by dint of the fact that he had had tea-bags somewhere in his case. Although I did not realize it then, reverberations caused by the affair of the missing Lapsang Souchong were to hang in the air for a considerable time.

When an article devoted to the wines of the Rhône appeared in *The Times* a few weeks later, Mr Graham studiously avoided any reference to my activities in that field, a total boycott that he was to pursue rigorously for years to come. The idea of trying to retrieve the situation became a sort of challenge, but all attempts at friendly overtures were always smartly rebuffed. Just when I was about to abandon these hopelessly unrewarding efforts, I suddenly remembered that the only time on that fateful evening at Hinckes Mill House that *The Times* wine writer had shown any animation, the one point in the evening when he had actually deigned to smile, had been when he had lovingly described the charm and beauty of the Charterhouse, his London home.

I had been intrigued to learn of this medieval foundation, an elegant institution where elderly single gentlemen might live out their last days among splendid ancient buildings and the fragrant blossoms of old-world gardens – just a few hundred yards away from the bustle and vulgarity of Smithfield Market, and facing the classic façade of the Henry VIII gateway of Bart's, St Bartholomew's Hospital. Resolving to make one final attempt to mollify the man, I telephoned Andrew Graham, asking to take up the half-made invitation to view the Charterhouse he had inadvertently let slip at our first meeting nearly three years earlier. Obviously surprised at my temerity in telephoning, he hesitantly agreed – becoming more positively affirmative when I assured him that I would take up a minimum of his time.

At this, our first physical encounter since the original meeting, we eyed each other tentatively as we muttered forms of greeting. Evincing every sign that it would be a painful nuisance, Mr Graham offered to make me coffee; I declined politely. We looked around the enormously attractive courtyards, then ambled through the gardens, where I admired massed banks of cottage garden summer flowers, and observed the propped-up boughs of an ancient mulberry tree. I managed to restrict our desultory conversation to bland generalities, only voicing my pleasure in the peaceful surroundings – never mentioning wine. At the end of forty minutes (the length of time we had agreed upon), I began some words of gratitude and prepared for swift departure. Mr Graham then wished to delay me, to prolong the conversation – he *even* offered me a glass of Manzanilla – but I judged departure prudent, and hurried off the scene. As I passed through an archway hard against the mulberry tree, Mr Graham's tremulous tones followed, demanding to be informed whether or not I was still an active wine merchant. I nodded affirmation as I stepped out into the square.

That evening Andrew telephoned, asking me to verify various facts and figures pertaining to the Rhône. Our conversation lasted for an hour, as I did my best to impart all that he wished to know. The following Saturday's *Times* carried a remarkably informative article that dealt in exquisite and arcane detail with the most esoteric wines of the Rhône. The last paragraph indicated (with a warmth that took my breath away) that all these delectable oddities were purchasable from Yapp. Sadly, I was unable to further the burgeoning friendship. Within a week Andrew Graham became ill and spent the last year or so of his life in a nursing home.

Burgundian Bacchanalia

Now it was time to go to France again. For the past six months I had been busily and vociferously claiming the status of a, if not *the*, leading specialist in the wines of Loire and Rhône: an epithet to which my entitlement was extremely dubious indeed – my field experience having consisted of that one day in the Loire Valley the previous year, and not so much as a single minute anywhere in the Rhône. The occasional heroic explorer – customers who succeeded in determinedly beating a path through the complex labyrinth of narrow country lanes that lay around Hinckes Mill House – tended to know France well; indeed, it was their affection for and knowledge of the vineyards of my chosen sectors that gave them the strength of purpose to make eventual landfall at my house.

When such a caller started to describe a *chai* or the vineyard of some particular grower in loving detail – the *vigneron*'s simple rustic cottage very near a ruined windmill, itself located a kilometre and a half into the hinterland of, say Vouvray – then proceeded to inquire as to my own acquaintanceship with the man or place, the temptation to pretend an intimate knowledge of the district in question was nigh-on irresistible, but had to be rejected with a rectitude that I was astonished to discover among my resources. At it turned out, my dismal ignorance did no harm whatsoever, because the visitor would luxuriate in such an unexpected opportunity to rehearse his own experiences, and delighted in the chance to enlighten his apparently eager listener . . . but my sense of being fraudulent, a veritable charlatan, mounted with each such encounter.

Then there was a further essential reason for mounting an expedition south through France. I had maintained my contact with Lichine – who can hardly have believed their good fortune: that first casual call at their premises in the Quai des Chartrons had been the precursor of quite a number of useful little shipments. At this time, a formal letter arrived: the official summons to an important soirée, to be held at Clos de Vougeot on the evening of Saturday 12 February

1969, a glittering occasion when I was to be elevated from the ranks of normal commonfolk, to be created a Chevalier du Tastevin, at the three hundred and forty-eighth *chapitre* of the Confrérie, a ceremony designed to celebrate the *renouveau et d'amitié Franco–Suisse*. Well, any excuse for a party, thought I, suppressing a passing thought that Swiss postulants for the heady honour must be somewhat thin upon the ground that season, as I hastily scribbled an enthusiastic letter of acceptance.

Michael was also invited to participate in the general festivities, to become a *confrère* too, so off we merrily went. The people at Lichine had suggested a certain hotel on the road between Beaune and Dijon, on the outskirts of Nuits Saint Georges, as an agreeable place to stay. Our room on the second floor was indeed acceptable. A recuperative nap after the fatigues of the journey proved to be impracticable, because the rear of the establishment was in the process of being repointed by a most industrious hammer-tapping dwarf of a stone-mason, so we soldiered on to Beaune, to make contact with our 'go-between', the *courtier* who masterminded Lichine's Burgundian estate-bottling operation. A couple of mildly uncomfortable hours then ensued, with the inherent language difficulties presenting the major hurdle. It was with distinct sighs of relief that we finally embarked upon the evening's excursion – pausing briefly at the hotel to don *le smoking*; obligatory for the impending entertainment.

Clos de Vougeot is staggeringly impressive – would be so to even the most recalcitrant of Rechabites; the setting for the evening's function was fabulously perfect, as we motored up to the château's feudal doorway, past lantern-lit, precisely aligned rows of leafless vines. More than four hundred immaculately turned-out guests milled around the courtyard and the great hall, dwarfed by the immensity of the awesomely massy beams of vast medieval wine presses. Champagne *brut* was being dispensed with admirable liberality – presumably to inculcate a sense of relaxed well-being before a lengthy harangue of welcome made by the portly *grand maître*, guarded by the members of the Grand Council of the Order, all togged out in a colourful pastiche of medieval robes.

The most delightful surprise upon our arrival at the château had been that our host, and godfather for the *intronisation*, was none other than the managing director of Lichine, a somewhat saturnine and taciturn ex-bank manager; a greater delight lay in the fact that this important personage was accompanied by an extremely attractive and vivacious South African girl whom Michael and I had enjoyed meeting in passing during our first sortie to Bordeaux. Not only was Lesley an amusing and aesthetic asset to any party, she had the decided advantage of being bilingual, so she was able to alert us when the harangue drew to its close. The ceremony of half a dozen postulants' election began ... and what an absurdly theatrical farrago of spurious medievalism it turned out to be – the flounced and beruffed robes, frequent fanfares on a bevy of heraldic horns and trumpets – yet ultimately the performance was curiously impressive and, finally, quite moving. When my turn came, I swore the oath in Middle French with some conviction and considerable gusto (fortified by the champagne, no doubt), was suitably honoured when dubbed upon the shoulder with a shillelagh-like vine-wood cudgel of a sceptre, quaffed the ceremonial cup with distinct abandon and, finally, took delivery of a rolled-up illuminated manuscript – the certificate and symbol of my enrolment into this brotherhood of wine.

The banquet that followed was truly amazing. Just the logistics of producing passable food for four to five hundred people crammed together at long tables in the dungeon-like cellars of Clos de Vougeot (a fire officer's nightmare, one would have thought; but perhaps a French *sapeur-pompier* is made of sterner stuff than his British counterpart) are mind-boggling enough; that each of the six courses should be marvellously delicious and, where appropriate, elegantly presented on really hot plates (rare enough in even the best French restaurants) was wonderful to witness. The *traiteur*'s performance that night was formidable to behold; it certainly knocked spots off anything in which I had been privileged to participate at Dewsbury Town Hall.

Les gentils porcelets et le jambon persillé dijonaise, relevés de bonne moutarde forte de Dijon were accompanied by a generous tidal wave of *bourgogne blanc* 1964 *frais et gouleyant. Les filets de sole au Meursault-humidifiés* came with a liberal sample of the wine in which they had been cooked, a Meursault-Charmes 1966, *subtil et bouqueté,* or so the menu said. By then we were quite in the mood for red wine; it came in the guise of Monthélie 1962, *soyeux et prenant* – the liquid partner to *le jambon braisé morvandelle.* The wine waiters – all *cavistes* to a man, and attired for the occasion in basic cellar uniform, the chief and essential component of which is the beret, hung at jaunty Gallic angle – dispensed the Beaune Premier Cru 1962 as though desperately trying to empty out a wine lake, so *le fricassée de poulardes de Bresse aux morilles* was welcomed as much for its absorbent qualities as for its innate excellence. *Les bons fromages de Bourgogne et d'ailleurs* were reinforced by a Mazis-Chambertin 1964 *de memorable lignée*: a rich, deep crimson beauty of a wine that very nearly turned me into a 'burgundy man' on the spot, just about converted me from being the fraudulent claret lover who had no business whatsoever to be luxuriating in all this marvellous Burgundian hospitality.

Boutehors turned out to be the pudding, or delicate dessert: *l'escargot en glace et les poires Clos de Vougeot*, accompanied by *les petits fours*. The alcoholic *coup de grâce* was administered in the form of Vieux Marc de Bourgogne *or* Prunelle de Bourgogne; by then my ability to make sensible decisions was grievously impaired – so I took a glass of each. The menu promised that these *digestifs*, taken with black coffee, would *fort idoines à stimuler vapeurs subtiles du cerveau* but, regrettably, at that late stage of the proceedings my poor brain was long past any possibility of recognizing or appreciating subtlety or nuance.

The whole glorious feast had been noisily punctuated by the raucous singing of the Confrérie's choir, the notorious Cadets de Bourgogne, whose lyrics were, I strongly suspected, not conspicuous for their subtlety either – judging by side-splitting guffaws of the Francophone members of our party. The din began to quieten as fellow celebrants began to drift away, and when our slightly sinister host, the head man of Lichine, suggested a move to a *boite de nuit*, I had not the slightest clue what the fellow was talking about. However, I had most definitely conceived the strongest passion for the charming, talkative and devastatingly pretty South African girl; very little but unconsciousness was going to be allowed to prise me from her side.

Dijon boasted two night-clubs at that time; we visited both. From an archival point of view, it is unfortunate that I was not in an ideal state to be able to make careful observation of this totally new experience but, I as far as I can now recall, I much preferred the Wild West Saloon; the music was more jolly and the waitresses looked particularly fetching in their minuscule cowgirl outfits.

It was probably round about then that the evening (or, rather, early morning) began to fall apart. Michael began to make signals of distinct alarm as I moved slowly, inch by inch, around the tiny dance floor – using Lesley's kindness in giving me support as a particularly heaven-sent pretext for drawing ever closer. The *courtier* from Beaune, his somewhat hirsute *épouse*, and the dark-featured managing director might have appeared to an alarmist to be positively glowering at me as we slowly glided (admittedly rather lurchingly) past their table; but they returned their attentions to the bottle of Chivas Regal fast enough as we continued to circumnavigate the floor.

At the moment when I was trying to press further my point about the wisdom and desirability of our taking a stroll around the fascinating streets of Dijon – so as to examine the heavenly constellations which would, without doubt, look so different when seen so much further south than Mere, not to say appear spectacularly unusual compared with the view from the vantage points of South Africa – strong and, considering the lateness of the hour, reasonably well-functioning arms separated me from my charming partner. The party appeared to be over, and terse 'goodnights' were exchanged.

As we tried to work out how to get into our car, Michael elaborated his theory that I had been behaving disgracefully in attempting to seduce (and that appallingly obviously) our host's young mistress. Ten days later, when I saw the many magnificent rooms of Lesley's designer-furbished apartment in the most fashionable district of Bordeaux, I had to accept my brother's sagacity and the truth of his words: even the fastest shorthand-typing does not attract *that* sort of salary, even in Bordeaux. When I saw the same apartment featured in *House and Garden* the following year, I merely felt rather silly.

Somehow, and I would prefer not to speculate how, we finally located the hotel. As previously arranged, a door had been left open, but progress to the staircase, necessarily through the restaurant, was a slow and noisy business, hampered as we were by darkness. I fear that the waiters had to reset at least a few of the tables later in the day. When we finally agreed which *was* our bedroom door, Michael then discovered that he had lost the key – which probably lay in the mud of the car park at Clos de Vougeot. A brainwave occurred to me: the mason had been using a rustic sort of ladder for his afternoon activities. In the end, most reluctantly, Michael agreed that he was fractionally the more sober. I sat upon the corridor floor, head against the door, and promptly went to sleep.

Later he claimed that it had proved difficult to arouse me, but being a lightish sort of sleeper, I cannot imagine how that could be; eventually I became aware of scrabbling noises and urgent whispers . . . coming through the door. How typically inefficient and inconsiderate of a French hotelier, I mused as I crawled along the corridor looking for the stairs, to have bedroom doors that cannot be unlocked from the inside of the room. What blandishments and encouragements my saintly brother employed, what pullings and pushings he administered, to get me up to and through the window on the second floor, I cannot now imagine, but it must have taken an effort bordering on the superhuman. We bade each other goodnight, and became unconscious in a flash.

When Michael persuaded me to awake next morning by the final expedient of confiscating the bedclothes, I was horrified to see the precipitous height of our nocturnal route to bed. A new and difficult factor was that the instrument of our deliverance had been repossessed by the gnome-like artisan: the stonemason had pinched the ladder. What special overtime rates was the hotel owner paying this master craftsman to start work at 7 a.m. on a Sunday? Our situation appeared impossible. Shouts and gesticulations at the wretched workman brought cheery waves of greeting as he continued at the laborious task in hand. At that moment came divine inspiration; for the first time in my life a French word that I would have sworn I had never previously heard before flashed into my head. 'A-shell, a-shell,' I hoarsely cried, 'A-shell, a-shell,' I cried again. Slowly a look of comprehension flitted across the mason's wrinkled features – *échelle* is what he heard, and that is what he now climbed off and brought over to our window.

Michael lost the vote again, thus being elected to search out the hotelier (or *hotelière*, as she eventually turned out to be) to borrow a spare key or pass key to expedite our release. A previous occupant of our room had mislaid the spare key prior to our arrival, he breathlessly explained, when once more at the ladder top; the only pass key was in the closely guarded custodianship of *la patronne* who did not live on the premises, and was thought unlikely to put in an appearance much before midday. That Michael had been mischievously misinformed, we soon realized; as I was handing down the second suitcase to the mason's willingly proffered hands, the lady in question walked round the corner. She did not bat an eyelid at our bizarre mode of exit – her quarrel was not with us; she paused to throw a gracious smile in our direction, before verbally savaging the miserable workman. In as much as we were able to understand the torrent of shrill abuse, it appeared that the fellow had been overpunctilious in his zeal to complete the job; it had been, the virago declared in strongest terms, an error to have commenced his labours at such an unseasonably early hour, to the detriment of her paying guests' unbroken sleep. Tirade over and honour, presumably, satisfied, the woman's good humour returned; her countenance became sunnier and more relaxed as she accompanied us round to the front of the building where, in the hallway, she installed herself at her usual seat of custom, the *caisse*, where we promptly paid . . . and fled.

The day could only get better, and it did . . . eventually. A detour west, to visit the Abbey of Cluny, proved to have been a slight error on my part. Monastic remains are all very interesting (particularly so if you are *not* nursing the most monumentally forehead-splitting hangover of all time), but the reason I had insisted upon making the fifty-kilometre deviation from our carefully planned route was a determination to pay tribute to the celebrated Cluny tapestries – the ravishingly lovely *La Dame et l'Unicorne* series that looks utterly beguiling, even as reproduced on picture postcards. The old lady in the ticket booth patiently conveyed to us that this famous artwork, masterpiece of the Renaissance, was on permanent display 250 kilometres to the north – in Paris, to be precise; where the tapestries formed the pinnacle of the magnificent collection of the Musée de Cluny, opposite the Sorbonne. Anyway, being there, we kicked around the Abbey's ruins in desultory fashion, before resuming our original route south . . . to the Beaujolais.

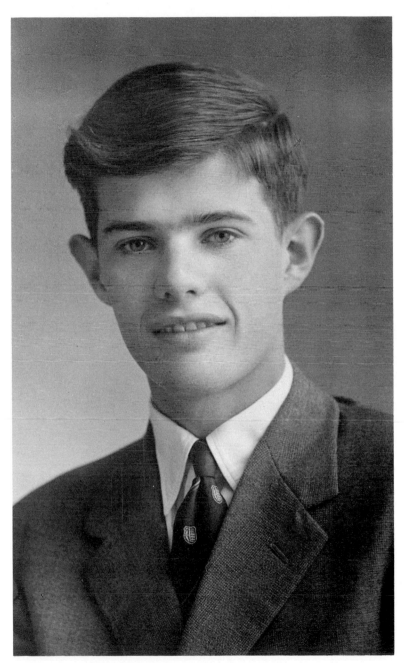

The author, Scarborough 1959

The Royal Hotel, Scarborough

Hinckes Mill House

The Old Brewery 'before' May 1973

The Old Brewery 'after' June 1973

Julian Bream

Travelling 'still', Sancerre

London Tasting 1972. From left to right: Pamela Vandyke Price, Robin
Yapp, Julian Jeffs Q.C. (standing), Cyril Ray

Elie Pagnon, Saint Pourçain-sur-
Sioule

Robert Cordier, Reuilly

Robert Jasmin

The day of the pig-killing, *chez* Chave

Beaujolais and the Rhône

We stopped in a village on the outskirts of Mâcon to buy the wherewithal for a simple picnic. Michael went off to the *boulangerie* to purchase their last *baguette*, while I selected some cheese, slices of *jambon cru*, butter, a little pot of *cornichons* and, most important of all, a bottle of Beaujolais, Saint Amour, in the village's *épicerie*. Our alfresco luncheon took place in the middle of a vineyard – not in the *appellation* of Saint Amour (which we had passed through earlier), but further on, in Juliénas. We must have presented an unusual, if not bizarre, spectacle to passing motorists, enveloped in our overcoats (although the sun was shining brightly, the air carried a chilly nip) but proudly sporting our insignias as fully paid-up, fully registered, members of the Confrérie des Chevaliers du Tastevin: around our necks we wore the bright red and gold-striped ribbons that support a silver tasting-cup, a *tastevin*.

A muddy, battered Citroën *deux chevaux* halted by the roadside, but not, on this occasion, so that its occupants might gawp at crazy foreigners; the driver, who was alone, approached us through the rows of vines. A young man in his twenties, he was grinning broadly with unmistakably friendly intent; in halting broken English only marginally better than our French, he explained that he had observed the GB plate on our equally mud-splattered Volvo. A week's holiday in England a year or so before had left him with indelible memories, coupled with an ineradicable passion for all things English.

We chatted with the lad as best we could – feeling incredibly foolish in our collarettes and *tastevins*, but our account of the previous evening's ceremony seemed to interest him greatly, definitely struck a chord. As evident wine lovers, were we thoroughly conversant with *all* the *vignobles* of Beaujolais, he asked, thoughtfully eyeing the by now empty bottle of Saint Amour? Upon our instantly disclaiming any personal knowledge of the vineyards that surrounded us, our new friend declared that there was nothing for it but to put ourselves completely in his hands: he would regard it as *un privilège immense* to undertake our education in the nuances of Beaujolais.

Feeling mildly astonished by this strange turn of events, we followed the *deux chevaux* to the pretty village of Lancié, two kilometres west of Romanèche-Thorin. Rolande's parents, Fernand and Minouche Sellier, seemed remarkably unsurprised when we drove into their courtyard, as did Rolande's charming wife, Sabine, and her attractive sister, Chantal. Our attempts to explain away our sudden appearance were rendered much easier by the excellence of the young women's English. While we retold the story of our Clos de Vougeot escapade, Fernand was busy pulling dusty bottles from his – for a Frenchman not professionally involved in wine – excellently comprehensive cellar, while Minouche had gone to get some spicy home-made *saucisson* to act as foil to the wine.

We could not have possibly fallen better; the whole delightful family were really keen on wine, and their knowledge, particularly Fernand's, of the background of the wines of their region made them the best mentors imaginable on the delights of good Beaujolais. My headache began to vanish as we tasted the best part of a dozen interesting bottles that Fernand had by now lined up upon the cellar table. When that good man was absolutely certain that we had absorbed as much information about those delicious wines (and as much wine) as possible, he announced that we would all now set out to carry out further research in the field.

A considerable research, made in great depth, it turned out to be! With Rolande at the driving wheel, we sped merrily from Beaujolais village to village, stopping at each and every *cave coopérative*, sparing not a single one from our attentions. As Sunday afternoons are when the entire population of the Beaujolais, and what seems like a good half of the citizenry of Lyons, makes the same highly agreeable peregrination, each *cave* was packed with a dense throng of thirsty French humanity, each individual intent upon organizing the refilling of his glass, then promptly emptying it so that the process could begin again, and so on *ad infinitum*, or at any rate until someone in the party decided that it was high time to move along to the next village, to recommence the performance there. It was interesting how frequently we ran into the same people as the afternoon progressed: they began to seem like old acquaintances.

Given the enthusiastic and dedicated way these jolly folk tackled the serious task of quality control of the region's famous product, and given the sudden tight corners and numerous hairpin bends, it seemed astonishing that the lanes between the villages were not rendered totally impassable by mounting piles of wrecked vehicles. St Vincent, patron saint of *vignerons*, must have been working extra shift to give these devotees of Beaujolais the benefit of his much needed protection – particularly, thank goodness, us. Rolande drove appallingly badly, and recklessly anti-socially, at as high a speed as Fernand's limousine could muster, turning his head at frequent intervals to address remarks to us, sitting in terror on the back seat, while rattling towards the next rapidly approaching vertiginous bend at an alarming rate of knots. The countryside seemed to be extraordinarily pretty as it flashed past the windows.

As Chénas succeeded Juliénas followed Moulin-à-Vent after Fleurie came behind Villie-Morgon, my alarm began to abate, so that I really began to enjoy this splendid notion, prevailing in the Beaujolais, of an ideal Sunday evening's perambulation. Now knowing absolutely everything that it could be remotely possible to know about the *vignobles* of the Beaujolais (not an iota of which I could recall the following morning), we whizzed back, in Rolande's inimitable fashion, to Lancié.

Our protestations of gratitude and moves to depart were brusquely waved aside: the goose was a particularly fine specimen that would easily serve to feed us all, provided that Minouche were quickly to augment the vegetables, prepare some extra *cèpes*. While Mme Sellier did exactly that, and while the younger women went to make up two beds in the *grenier*, a loft beneath the pantiled roof, it was solemnly agreed that the only proper place for the menfolk was undoubtedly the cellar, so that was where we installed ourselves for the next hour or so.

Fernand was a genuine wine enthusiast with a knowledgeable interest in all the wines of France. I seem to recollect us participating in a 'crash-course' in the finer points of burgundy – probably in honour of our *tastevins*, which seemed to have mysteriously reappeared about our necks. The goose was indeed a fine one; the simple rustic repast absolutely splendid . . . and the wines just got better as the evening progressed. We slept soundly. Next morning, obviously determined to give us 'indelible memories, coupled with an ineradicable passion for all things *French*', our cheerful hosts had risen early, to prepare a *vigneron*'s breakfast: as assortment of sausages, game pâté, bewildering permutations of ham, and a tasty grilled *bifteck*, all washed down with bumpers of Lancié Beaujolais.

We have kept in touch with these wonderfully kind people ever since that unforgettable first encounter; I am deeply grateful that I have been able to pass other equally splendid days in their boisterous, infectious company when travelling towards the Rhône. Tragically, Rolande died in an accident several years ago; not, as might well have been supposed, in a head-on confrontation with another vehicle while charging with his habitual gay abandon through the narrow lanes of his beloved Beaujolais. The propeller of a speedboat decapitated him while he was swimming in the sea.

Nowadays I find that visiting the enchanting villages of the Beaujolais has lost a great deal of its savour, now that I drive along the little roads sedately, without the marvellous company and the vigorous sparkle of my original guide and erstwhile friend.

Our first properly professional appointment of the trip was in Ampuis, first wine village of the Northern Rhône, thirty miles south of that capital of gastronomy, Lyons. On the west bank of the Rhône and straddling the busy RN86 (a minor, but traffic-crammed road, notorious for its many bends, that runs beside the river from here virtually to the sea), Ampuis is delightfully typical of the rather old-fashioned viticultural villages of the Ardèche; there is a distinct feeling that, in many ways, time has stood still. The distinguished wine of the *appellation* is called Côte Rôtie, made from the grape variety found throughout the Northern Rhône, the classic Syrah – thought to have been indigenous in these parts for more than two thousand years, legacy of the earliest Phocaean Greek immigrants who used the Rhône as a passageway into Europe around the sixth century BC.

The vineyards themselves were remarkable: dizzily stacked terraces (many so narrow as to support two or three rows of vines only) retain a dubious hold upon the vertiginous cliff face by means of drystone walls; at once we appreciated the immense labour which their cultivation entailed. At the time of that first visit, in 1969, the terraces presented distinct signs of decline and impending dereliction. Labour had become increasingly costly, and mechanical means of cultivation were clearly out of the question on such an impossible terrain; the wine-drinking world was still besotted by the more famed charms of burgundy and claret, to the neglect and exclusion of all other wines, no matter what their excellence or value. It then seemed perfectly possible that these amazingly precipitous vineyards might continue to decline. Our rendezvous was with a vociferous champion and defender of this apparently failing cause, a M. Bathier, manager of Vidal-Fleury, one of the two important *négociant* houses in Ampuis.

Ralph, my advertising 'partner' in London, was UK agent for Vidal-Fleury, and had gladly furnished me with the warmest of introductions. The establishment was by the roadside at the entry to the village, angular white-painted stucco buildings typical of the 1930s, when they were constructed. M. Bathier's office, into which we were immediately ushered, had an even older-fashioned flavour imparted by its furniture and fittings, and the patina of age. There was something very charming about the shabby *fin de siècle* comfort of the office, with its worn and scuffed leather-upholstered armchairs and ornate ormolu Empire clock, forever standing at five minutes to five.

M. Bathier was friendly and helpfully informative, patient in the extreme with my patent lack of knowledge, and wonderfully long-suffering with our (well, *my*) woefully inadequate grasp of his elegant language. The French tend to treat their tongue as a valued museum piece; to have to listen to clumsy queries couched in ill-constructed and halting sentences, wildly mispronounced in the worst imaginable English (and Algerian) accents must have been acutely distressing for a sensitive and civilized Frenchman like M. Bathier.

After giving a brief but vivid description of the *appellation*'s history, he proposed a quickish tour of the vineyards' precipitous slopes. The terraces bristled with the stout chestnut stakes which serve to support the luxuriant growth of summer; now, in February, the vines had recently been pruned, were dormant and leafless, and looked, well, rather unimpressive. The cycle of the *vigneron*'s annual activities was recounted in useful detail. When the winter chill had penetrated our overcoats, M. Bathier returned us to the warmth of his friendly office. During our absence a pleasant-looking assembly of bottles had been set upon the desk, so that we might taste the Vidal-Fleury range.

Ralph could not have been accurately described as a wine buff, or as an enthusiastic devotee of the noble product of the grape. He had entered the wine trade by default, I suspected, in lieu of any other possibilities and, after all, it *was* his family's firm. Reasonably astute at commerce, he might well have been as happy dealing in cabbages or coal – though it had to be admitted that he had displayed unmistakable signs of enthusiasm when we had polished off the Taylor's '27. Quite in what manner this important Northern Rhône agency had come his way had never been related – to me, at any rate – but I had formed the distinct impression that the whole thing had happened by lucky accident, some form of nepotism – probably a chance encounter with an old ex-military chum who happened to know someone . . . something along those lines, I rather thought.

Such was his dynamism and deep interest in the subject that, while Ralph had undoubtedly registered the fact that his principals in Ampuis made a red wine called Côte Rôtie, knew of and imported their excellent version of Hermitage, was perhaps less secure as to what Châteauneuf-du-Pape was doing on his list, yet he had never even *realized* that his famous suppliers produced a virtually complete range of Rhône wines so, of course, had been unable to inform me on the matter. There on the ink-stained, leather-topped desk stood a clutch of bottles bearing the names of wines that were a mystery to me or that, if vaguely heard of, had certainly never come my way.

Our host nonchalantly drew the corks of arcane unknowns such as Lirac and Gigondas, *white* Châteauneuf-du-Pape and Muscat de Beaumes-de-Venise, as well as examples of Ralph's mainstream imports. It was a thrilling moment . . . and the wines were very good indeed. We discussed the possibility of my persuading our mutual contact to supply me with these marvellous new discoveries, an idea with which M. Bathier happily concurred.

Our linguistic ability seemed to take a distinct turn for the better as the tasting session proceeded, and M. Bathier also seemed to relax – so much so that, despite the tremendous verbal battering that the poor fellow had had to endure over the previous two hours, he courteously inquired as to any arrangements we might have made for lunch. We easily succeeded in conveying our complete availability.

As he leaned across the desk for the familiar red-bound *Guide Michelin*, M. Bathier asked how well acquainted we might be with . . . La Pyramide.

La Pyramide! No one with even a minimal interest in good food or good things French could *not* know of this famed temple of gastronomy. Its founder died nearly thirty years ago, but such was his profound influence that many well-known restaurants in France exist because of Fernand Point, created by devoted disciples who learned their art at his hands. Even the street, formerly named for the imposing Roman obelisk (a *spina*, one of the two turning posts of the Roman hippodrome) that stands there – the Pyramide – has been renamed rue Fernand Point, and the restaurant is certainly referred to by its devotees as *chez* Point.

We attempted to stifle our rising excitement, to look composed, as we quietly murmured that, for some inexplicable reason, we had yet to make the pilgrimage and that we would be far from averse to toying with a dish or two at that particular eating-house. With incredible slowness, as though luncheon *chez* Point might be an ordinary, everyday sort of occurrence, M. Bathier quietly thumbed his *Michelin*, looking for the telephone number, so that Mme Point might be alerted to our imminent arrival.

A *fermeture hebdomadaire* is the 'day off', the day when a restaurant or hotel is shut; this day, this Monday, M. Michelin informed us, was La Pyramide's *fermeture hebdomadaire*; the place would be totally and incontrovertibly shuttered up, locked up, closed for business. We were very brave and raised somewhat watery smiles of agreement when M. Bathier suggested that we rough it, take pot luck, at some modest establishment down river at Condrieu. Le Beau Rivage merits a mere two stars in the Michelin galaxy.

The rest of the day is a blurred but happy memory; the Rhône hurtled powerfully past the terrace as dish succeeded delectable dish. We were fearfully shocked by the sheer extravagance of our host commanding that six different Vidal-Fleury wines be brought to the table for our delectation: I dearly wished to push the corks back into near-full bottles, for the benefit of their solace that evening at a hotel further downstream. We parted from M. Bathier, muttering garlicky, and probably quite incomprehensible, gratitudes for a generous and illuminating day; then, through the haze and language barrier, we vaguely realized that this good and worthy person was asking us to call again upon our next visit to the Rhône.

Michael was unable to join me the following year, so I was alone as I sped straight for Ampuis, Vidal-Fleury and M. Bathier. Towards midday (five minutes to five, according to the ormulu clock) M. Bathier casually asked if I was at liberty to join him for lunch; was I conversant with a neighbourhood hostelry called La Pyramide? He reached for his *Guide Michelin* . . .

In point of fact, my entire trip had been planned so that I might be in *that* office on a Tuesday rather than a Monday. As I expressed a polite interest in any Michelin three-star restaurant that might exist in the vicinity, it was evident that the relevant entry was being closely scrutinized. At some point during the year that had passed, Mme Point had changed the fixed custom of nearly half a century, and had elected to alter the weekly *fermeture hebdomadaire* from time-hallowed Monday . . . to Tuesday.

I am forced to confess that we ate extremely well at the one-star Hôtel Bellevue, across the river from Condrieu (indeed, that establishment has since shared my allegiance for overnight accommodation with the Beau Rivage on the opposite bank in all the intervening years). Again the reassuring phalanx of Vidal-Fleury bottles for appraisal and assessment; perhaps a slightly more comprehensible contribution to the conversation came from me. We parted on terms of great amity, with my proffered deep-felt thanks. Eventually I *was* to get to La Pyramide, but that is another story.

Upon my return from the earlier visit to Ampuis, I was astonished to find to what degree I had to cajole Ralph so as to get possession of my earnestly desired oddities, the Lirac and the Gigondas and the Muscat de Beaumes-de-Venise. A campaign of attrition finally won the day, coupled with a guarantee that I would liquidate any stocks within the period of six months; only upon my assurance that such would be the case did Ralph finally relent, and then only with the most enormous reluctance would he agree to add ten cases each of white Châteauneuf-du-Pape and the others to his next shipment of Côte Rôtie.

In the event, a reshipment was necessary well before the time limit's expiration and, within the year, Ralph's main wholesale list carried all the previously resisted newcomers and they were figuring in his national advertising. The main lesson for me was that such esoteric wines truly existed out there in the vineyard areas, and reconfirmed my earliest suspicion that these delightful rarities might indeed be marketable.

Apart from having the worst row with my brother (who objected increasingly hysterically to my insistence on a dawn start each morning, who complained of fatigue and exhaustion, and who even made a fairly determined bid for freedom – suddenly claiming to have urgent business somewhere in the Alps, but who was eventually mollified by my agreeing that a 9 a.m. departure would, I reluctantly supposed, be in order) that I could ever remember, my last *really* cogent memory of the great wine trek of 1969 was of our visit to Chapoutier.

Ronnie Scott of Hellmers had arranged a powerful introduction to this significant *négociant* house. Unfortunately, I appeared to have got the day wrong; what with all those early reveilles, we seemed to have gained an extra day. At any rate we caused embarrassed consternation when we presented ourselves at the Chapoutier main offices in a side street of Tain l'Hermitage a day earlier than anticipated. We had not actually observed it as we mounted the outside staircase to knock upon the door, but the gable end above the doorway carried a tiny flagstaff; Chapoutier considered it to be absolutely *de rigueur* to fly the national flag of any expected visitor. The flag that we had failed to see that morning was that of West Germany. When we left the premises for luncheon, the British pennant was hanging limply from the pole – we only knew it was there when it was courteously pointed out to us as we passed beneath.

The unfortunate personnel of Chapoutier were condemned by our thoughtless early arrival to spend the rest of the day changing the flags around and organizing our itinerary so that we and the German party (who at one point we distinctly discerned on the far side of the place Taurobole, before they were whisked around a corner out of sight) never met. Apparently, our genial hosts were under the impression that any confrontation between the two parties was likely to lead to some unpleasant incident, a sort of final outbreak of the Second World War, so we never met the opposition, but twice saw the Union Jack being jerkily hoisted as we came round a corner.

In a way, the meeting was historic. Presumably because of an undue pressure on the establishment's reception committee resources we were destined to meet M. Chapoutier *père*, an elegant and charming man who had recently retired. M. Marc Chapoutier entertained us nobly and captivated us completely; the company was indeed fortunate to possess an ambassador of such calibre. The venue for this, the first of many luncheons (taken ever afterwards in the company of Marc's son and successor, an ebulliently Napoleonic and very amusing Max), I cannot now remember; the Hôtel du Commerce perhaps, or the Hôtel de Paris on the other side of the Rhône, in Tournon. I have no doubt that the food was delicious and certainly the wines would have been magnificent – but none within a light year of the treat that was to follow.

Following a tour of all the different Chapoutier premises scattered through the town (our progress carefully programmed, to avert any possible danger of a clash between Teuton and Briton) – a visit to the main *chai*, to the cooperage, to the bottling line, to barrel-stacked storehouses, and an excursion up the hill of Hermitage itself – we retraced our steps to our starting point, passing a now breeze-blown Union Jack as we entered through the door.

As a supreme compliment, and as the culmination of a fascinating tasting, our distinguished elderly guide had arranged for the abstraction from a treasure house of venerable vintages of an antique bottle, a hand-blown bottle, of Hermitage Blanc 1929. This historic remnant of a legendary vintage had grown amber with age, had lost all acidity, to become soft and almost sweet, but remained defiantly viable – a first enormously significant demonstration of the ageing potential of the great vintages of the Northern Rhône, red *or* white. My introduction to the vineyards of the Northern Rhône, Les Côtes-du-Rhône Septentrionales, had been enormously educational and highly memorable. I began to feel that my apprenticeship had really commenced.

Ray to the Rescue

It was during these exciting, stirring times that Edmund Penning-Rowsell resurfaced in my life, making good his shouted promise to remain in contact. What was for me virtually a royal command invited me to pass a weekend in the Penning-Rowsell household in a village near Oxford. I instantly accepted.

I felt rather nervous as I sought out the house, but Meg, Mrs Penning-Rowsell, is an infinitely sweet person, who soon put me at my ease. Tension remounted as the hour of dinner approached. Edmund is considered by his colleagues and acquaintances to be noticeably abstemious, some say practically abstinent, which is a remarkable attribute for one who is numbered in the illustrious ranks of the wine trade (by virtue of his long-term chairmanship of the International Exhibition Co-operative Wine Society); he sacrifices volume for quality: the modest amount of wine that he partakes is of a high order. As I had feared, dinner proved to be a frightfully formal occasion, smart older people being my fellow guests. Thimblefuls of fino did little to lower barriers, or to induce in me a propensity for brightly intellectual conversation as we bravely attempted to appear madly social. Dinner was served. The ambience was lovely, a polished mahogany table top setting off ancestral silver to perfection, glass goblets glinting in the candlelight; three plain glass decanters holding richly red, translucent wine decorated the table's centre.

My forebodings had been accurate, my apprehension fully justified . . . because it was towards me that Edmund slid the first decanter, with the frightful suggestion that I should assay the vessel's contents, and *then* give the attentive assembly of gentlepersons the benefit of my considered views. Horror! Tremblingly I poured out a modicum of wine; hesitantly, I then picked up the glass with nerveless fingers. I did not, thank heavens, repeat a little mishap that had befallen me once before when, trying nonchalantly to look master of the situation, I had lowered my nose into a near-brimful glass, with the object of sniffing and analysing its contents, whereupon my delicate inhalation had siphoned half the glass's contents up my left nostril, causing me to cough and to splutter the excellent wine over all bystanders. No, in these awesome surroundings I delicately breathed in the wine's aroma, its gorgeous bouquet.

There will never ever be another opportunity in my life to appear to be so faultlessly in control of the 'find the claret' game, bane of wine merchants' lives. At no stage actually tasting the beverage in question, simply smelling, I gravely pronounced it to be claret . . . and no mean one at that. For five and a half minutes, after briskly eliminating the Médoc proper as its source, I hummed, ha'd and hesitated around the borders dividing Saint Emilion from Pomerol, making tentative little sorties, first in one direction then the other: 'Saint Emilion', I gravely but firmly announced to the expectant circle around the table. Discerning the vintage was the next major concern, and I ran dizzy rings round the early 1950s – 1952, 1953, 1955 and back again – for a full four minutes, voicing the pros and cons each time, before I was prepared to state my final unequivocal conviction that here we had a fine example of 1955. Fifty seconds of nose back into beaker, then, after what seemed to me to have been a forty-minute session (but was probably truly the ten minutes that I have described) I announced my full and final decision, still with wine-untainted mouth: the crimson liquid in the decanter and in the glass before me was, I pronounced . . . Château Figeac 1955.

Gracefully accepting the plaudits of a vociferously admiring audience, I somehow, in all the excitement, forgot to communicate to these suddenly much more attractive and far more amiable people the rationale that lay behind my astonishing *tour de force*. At that first olfactory confrontation with what was obviously a magnificent wine, my stomach had begun to flutter and then gone on to heave. Going for the wildest but still the most obvious hunch, I had risked all on the vague recollection of the last time that a splendid wine had reduced me to gastric misery, the distant memory of the days when Château Figeac 1955 had been the least expensive beverage in my Exmouth cupboard.

Naturally enough, after a virtuoso performance like that, Edmund Penning-Rowsell never again asked for my opinion, erroneously assuming that I would always be correct.

Indeed, such was the standing that I had derived from the amazing feat that a second invitation to a weekend *chez* Penning-Rowsell arrived the following year. Far less apprehensive on this second occasion, I very much appreciated meeting my pleasant fellow diners. A distinguished professor of music from an Oxford college, Austrian by origin, was accompanied by his slightly blue-rinsed American wife. This time the aperitif consisted of eyeglassfuls of Dos Cortados, William and Humbert's excellent palo cortado. The American matron sweetly asked if Edmund would be so kind as to elucidate the special qualities of the wine; he acquiesced and began to speak.

It was a tremendous performance by any standard, a truly masterly exposition of the complexities and unique subtleties of palo cortado sherry in general, and of Dos Cortados in particular. To listen to my hero in full poetic flood was a marvellous and illuminating experience. I wished that the moment could continue for ever; for an opera enthusiast the equivalent might be to have the privilege of overhearing some favourite famous diva practising Bellini arias in her bath. All too soon, the exquisite recital sounded its ultimate melodic cadences. Utter silence ensued, lasting for several minutes; obviously the academic couple had been as deeply moved as I. Eventually, the spellbound peace was broken . . . by the Professor's spouse. 'Gee, Eddie,' she whispered, 'that was wonderful, and now I fully understand . . . you mean that a palo cortado sherry is more like a vermooth.'

Edmund was about to do me a great favour, although I did not know so at the time.

For reasons of nostalgia (and economy), Exmouth was the choice of venue for our family holiday in the summer of 1969, and a peaceful, relaxed 'bucket and spade on the sands' affair it was turning out to be, with sufficient unusual sunshine to cause interested comment. With time, for once, to peruse a newspaper, I idly turned the pages of the *Observer* at the breakfast table, looking for the wine column which was then in the masterly hands of a certain Mr Ray, who *always* wrote in a most amusing fashion.

Elizabeth Ray's adjacent article caught my eye: a tempting recipe for a tasty-sounding courgette soup (which I still intend to attempt, one day soon); her husband's space concerned itself with a brace of Yugoslavian wines, neither of which sounded half as interesting as the soup; then, after an enthusiastic appraisal of three sherries newly launched upon the market, he continued:

> Finally, a welcome to Yapp Brothers who, in a period when small individual firms of wine merchants are foundering, merging or being taken over, have had the courage to set up (in Mere, Wiltshire) as independent specialists in Rhône and Loire wines. They have no fewer than fifteen reds and whites at 15s or under, and their informative list is worth sending for.
>
> Cyril Ray

I was dumbfounded, astonished, flabbergasted . . . and thrilled! Cornflakes, and any other cereal, were declared redundant to the moment: the snap, crackle and pop were provided by a bottle of champagne (Roederer non-vintage) that I had prudently slipped into my case as a useful accessory in the event of an emergency such as this.

In the week that followed I sat on the beach in something of a daze, as several hundred of Ray's devoted disciples did exactly what he had instructed them to do, wrote to beg the favour of a copy of my list which was, it must be confessed, a fairly pathetic little effort, only saved from being an utter disgrace by the highly literate and most professional analyses of a couple of items from the skilled pens of Messrs Jeffs and Penning-Rowsell. Its only other saving grace was that the listed wares were, without question, made from genuine grapes, and grapes alone – so were *reasonably* potable *and* represented reasonable value.

My unfortunate father, by now retired from journalism, had made the error of volunteering to man the so-called office, so it was he who had to cope with ever-mounting drifts of mail, a positive avalanche of letters, through the ensuing weeks. The list had to be reprinted quickly – but at least that gave me a valuable opportunity to eliminate some of the grosser errors that littered too many of its pages. Subsequently, one or two of the recipients of the brochure even ordered wine: it began to seem as though I might be getting into business – at long last.

With some real, live *actual* correspondence to be dealt with, it seemed an appropriate moment at which to start to sort out the ancillary staffing of the enterprise. Michael happened to be on leave, so I summoned him to a conference. The hour was getting late and the level in the second bottle of champagne (intended to summon up the Muses) had fallen to a disconcertingly low level by the time that we felt that we had finally got the matter right. Resisting, with commendable strength of purpose, a compellingly strong urge to employ lower case ffs, we used the remnants of the bottle to celebrate the christening of my new and mythical secretary: Felicity Maw-Forbes had just been conceived, born and, unnervingly rapidly, attained her majority.

For the next eighteen months I typed out every single letter (and every single letter of each and every epistle) that issued from the so-called office of Hinckes Mill House. Using a single digit, my much abused forefinger, I bashed out every letter, either early in the morning, or after surgery hours (it was pretty astonishing that that sorely tried part of my anatomy did not become deformed as month followed month) on a battered Olivetti that could almost claim the status of an antique. My mother (my parents were by now living in the apartment above the surgery) developed a highly credible Felicity Maw-Forbes signature.

The system worked astoundingly well for at least the first year, but a nagging and slightly worrying problem began to develop in that my assumption of the persona of this sweet and attractive young creature was beginning to become so successful, the tenor of my missives so delightfully charming, that some of her more gallant correspondents began to write letters couched in terms distinctly more friendly than a normal business relationship strictly demanded. Some of the guilt must attach to me, of course, because I confess that I was unable to resist responding a *little* in similar vein. In just one or two cases the extremely rapid burgeoning of friendship became positively alarming.

Eventually, and with the greatest reluctance, it became necessary to dispense with the otherwise impeccable services of an unhappy Miss Maw-Forbes: mild mail-order flirtation with the customers was one thing, but I could not possibly countenance the hussy accepting dinner engagements or even, forbid the very thought, agreeing to weekend assignations at remotely situated country house hotels with any of my estimable clientele. Besides, I had never felt the least urge to dress up in women's clothes.

A somewhat tearful ex-employee decided (and, I must say, I thought *very* wisely) to start a new life – by emigrating to the Antipodes (where I gather that things have gone considerably better for her than they did in rural Wiltshire), apprising her many admirers of her sudden departure by means of a carefully worded letter (exquisitely typed) on the eve of her voyage.

Some magic was missing from the establishment when I again took up the reins of dealing with day-to-day correspondence. The only delighted party was my mother; the non-stop forging of Felicity's signature had begun to prey upon her nerves, and to cause her some uneasiness regarding her true identity.

My gratitude for Mr Ray's generously fulsome acknowledgement of my debut in the wine trade was obviously boundless, which sentiment I expressed to him with all the warmth and rapidity that I could muster. The niggling mystery as to how he was even aware of my very existence was easily solved: Edmund Penning-Rowsell had written to Cyril Ray, enclosing a copy of my meagre first list, outlining my ambitions, and tactfully but firmly suggesting that he might be persuaded to feel inclined to lend a helping hand. Naturally, I was extremely anxious to make the personal acquaintance of this important benefactor; in due course I was successful in engaging him and his wife to lunch with me at the Connaught on a mutually auspicious day.

For some reason – mostly shyness, I would imagine – I became queasily apprehensive as the moment of our arranged encounter drew nearer and nearer. As I sat unhappily on the edge of a settee in the Connaught's bar, the realization swept over me that I had no way of recognizing Mr and Mrs Ray, because I had seen a photograph of neither, and had forgotten to ask for a description for identification purposes. Every five minutes I made a tour of the hotel's public rooms, carefully inspecting everyone around me, wondering whether the tall, almost emaciated man of distinction, garbed in grey overcoat, might be Mr Ray, or could he be the fellow slumped at the bar? In the event my worries were superfluous: a shortish, stoutish – but definitely *most* distinguished – gentleman in his mid-sixties stalked around the periphery of the bar, barking out 'Robin Yapp!',

'Robin Yapp!' at twenty-second intervals as he progressed around the room.

My foolish initial nervousness was swiftly superseded by pleasure as I made my presence known to an exceptionally pleasant couple; within no time whatsoever Cyril and Liz Ray succeeded in allaying my apprehensions. By the end of a splendid (but wickedly expensive) luncheon, what has been (for me, at any rate) a wonderful and enduring friendship was firmly in the course of construction.

It seemed somewhat surprising that Liz should choose to finish with prosaic bread-and-butter pudding when presented with the choice from a veritable cornucopia of exotic provender put at our disposal by an attentive Connaught management, but I should have guessed that her selection constituted research in the culinary field; the Connaught's receipt for an extremely elevated version of bread-and-butter pudding duly appeared in the columns of the *Observer* several weeks later. The accompanying wine article again extolled Yapp:

> Let me use my space to commend a new small specialist firm of wine shippers, run by enthusiasts: Yapp Brothers, Mere, Wilts, who sell (by the dozen) carefully picked wines only from the Rhône and the Loire, including some aristocratic estate-bottled Châteauneuf-du-Pape whites and reds at up to 30s or so, and such bargains as dry whites from the Loire at 13s and a Gigondas at 14s 6d. But send for their list, which is helpfully explanatory, and tell them I told you to.
>
> Cyril Ray

As I studied and restudied these (to me) jewelled words, and having called down fervently heartfelt blessings upon the head of this saintly person, I musingly reflected that there was undoubtedly nothing like going for overkill. The idea of mounting a press tasting in the metropolis gently began to form in the recesses of my mind.

Without any doubt, the wide dissemination of the news of my business's existence by wine journalists has contributed enormously to its modest success, so it seems an appropriate point at which to make the sincerest vote of thanks to these good friends for their great support, approbation and general encouragement over the last eighteen years. Britain is marvellously well endowed with intelligent, literate and knowledgeable wine writers whose columns amuse and inform us all in practically every newspaper and periodical in the land. These (on the whole) kind, but occasionally (when necessary) critical, viticultural scribes have certainly done their stuff by me.

What immediately became an annual event, my regular press tasting, gives the main opportunity to expose the journalists to the delights of any new wines garnered in the vineyards, and added to the list in the course of the intervening year, and to re-present old favourites that may be in danger of being eclipsed by the brash newcomers. Of course, there are other encounters with one or more of these estimable people on other occasions, in London or in Mere, through the rest of the year, but the big London tasting is the most important event, when one hopes that a maximum number of influential wine columnists will gather together to *look* at between twenty and thirty carefully selected samples. (I derive a simple pleasure from use of the word 'look': ordinary mortals drink wine, quaff it, knock it back by the bumper; dedicated wine lovers reverently taste the object of their affection; but members of the wine trade and wine journalists demurely *look* at the stuff – but you might be astonished at what an appreciable volume of wine can be made to evaporate simply by 'looking' at it.)

As a compliment to these worthy friends and colleagues, and to amuse them (*and* to lure them into the fold), one tries to come up with a new venue each time, a fresh location that is relatively easily accessible for everyone but pleasantly unusual. Achieving the right balance can sometimes be difficult but, on the whole, over the years, I have been fortunate in being able to come up with something novel and new. The Crane Kalman Gallery in Sloane Street was great fun – when we sampled the wines in an ambience of rustic antique Americana. The Garrick Club is always a friendly and hospitable milieu in which to assemble, where one can combine examination of the wines with that of the Garrick's splendid collection of eighteenth- and nineteenth-century theatrical paintings, the richly coloured Zoffanys adorning the walls.

One of the most original settings of all, for a recent tasting, was the Antiques Hall of that amazing emporium, something of a cult temple for its many *aficionados*, Thomas Goode's of South Audley Street, where the royals buy each others' wedding presents. On that upmarket occasion our enterprising and energetic hosts tricked out their two best show windows (where the two outsize china elephants normally hold court) with fabulously beautiful (and fabulously expensive) wine paraphernalia and drink-associated bibelots, crowning their efforts by helpfully emblazoning each showcase with the name of Yapp! A slightly bemused congregation of wine writers was served a delicious buffet on valuable porcelain plates, while the beverage wine was dispensed with reckless abandon into precious Waterford goblets. I was thankful that my journalist friends, who were evidently on very best behaviour in such awesome surroundings, behaved impeccably – nobody dropped *anything*.

Other places that have given a much appreciated home to London tastings include Prue Leith's excellent restaurant in Holland Park, where she fed us exceedingly well; the dramatic bottle-walled cellars of the Café Royal where we lunched magnificently somewhere beneath the pounding traffic of busy Regent Street, feeling exceptionally obligated towards the benevolent Sir Charles Forte who had paid for the feast; the Royal Society of Medicine's palatial town house headquarters, imposing Chandos House. I know that rival companies have favoured holding public relations functions on boats scudding up and down the Thames but, so far, no one seems to have thought of engaging the services of a fleet of hot air balloons . . . I *might* give that a try.

The first Yapp tasting in 1970 was in many ways the best, or certainly as successful as anything that has happened since, and the most marvellously perfect part about it was it was absolutely free and gratis – except for the tasting wines, of course. When I put my notion to him, Ralph saw sense in my reasoning; with remarkable promptitude, he agreed to let me stage the tasting in the highly appropriate surroundings of his Tooley Street cellars (carefully concealing the remaining bottles of Taylor's '27 before the journalists arrived). Furthermore he was prepared to organize a copious buffet luncheon at the company's expense . . . provided that at least half the wines on the tasting table were from his list. Naturally, I concurred at once.

It turned out to be almost the high spot of the season – although it somehow failed to gain recognition in 'Jennifer's Diary'; a galaxy of celebrities of wine journalism put in an impressive appearance – most probably because of my absolute anonymity, which may have made them think to check me out. Cyril Ray (of course), Pamela Vandyke Price, Julian Jeffs, Edmund Penning-Rowsell (although he seldom attends them nowadays: perhaps someone has alerted him to the fraudulence of my supposed claret expertise), Harry Yoxall, and so on: a most illustrious catalogue of names. Later, Ralph and I voted the affair an extremely satisfactorily high-scoring list; we thought to repeat the event at some time in the future.

At the re-run, the second London tasting two years later, an already declining relationship between us was hastened towards its demise by an unfortunate and most regrettable incident.

It so happened that the 1972 edition of the *Good Food Guide* had just been published on the very eve of the second tasting – on which occasion I had every intention of trying to dazzle what I hoped might be an even more numerous assembly of distinguished scribblers with the sheer quality of some new-found discoveries. In an inevitable state of pre-performance nerves, I had somehow failed to register the fact that the *Guide* was causing an exceptional furore by having printed what quickly became known in the wine trade as the 'list of the ten worst wines in the world'. In fact, the whole thing was intended as a sort of rule-of-thumb litmus test of restaurant wine lists: 'If the names noted below make up more than a quarter of any list, you need not seek further information, for it is unlikely to be forthcoming: drink the carafe wine (though you may regret even that) or beer, and escape as cheaply as you can.'

The second Yapp tasting was to take place, like the first, in the catacombs beneath London Bridge Station. In my excitement I had failed to realize that, with two of his best-selling products taking first and second place (by a considerable margin, unkind people might have thought) in the *Good Food Guide*'s scroll of infamy, my usually genial, agreeable host was not going to be *exactly* thrilled that morning when, on scanning my crumpled list of acceptances, he spotted the name of Christopher Driver, then editor of the aforesaid grievously offensive *Guide* (though, if the truth were known, the inflammatory passage in question bore the fairly unmistakable hallmark of Mr Ray's elegant circumlocution . . . but I forbore from pointing that out).

My friend's first thought was to issue a swiftly telephoned dictate to his lawyer, insisting that he attend the morning's session armed to the teeth with writs for libel. It was only with considerable blandishment and the most persuasive coaxing that Ralph could be dissuaded from pursuing that course of action. Eventually, Guards tie immaculately straightened, stiff upper lip firmly under control, the valiant man declared himself fully in control of his severely assaulted emotions. The tasting commenced.

For the best part of two hours I contrived to keep the two antagonists as far apart as was physically possible – putting the maximum yardage of the, fortunately, long bottle-strewn tasting table between them. At (what seemed to me) very long last, luncheon was announced. By this stage in the proceedings, the majority of the writer visitors were becoming rather jumpy; it is well known that journalists are sensitive folk, and they had begun to sense the strained atmosphere. Their unease was much compounded when they saw that the trestle luncheon tables were closely hemmed in by towering walls made up of hundreds of cartons of wine, all proudly displaying the legend 'La Flora Blanche' – undisputed number one on the *Good Food Guide*'s list of shame – surely no place for any self-respecting wine writer to be captured for posterity (or possibly for the tabloids) by the newly arrived professional photographer so thoughtfully summoned by our host.

Such is the ameliorating affect of good wine (when taken in *reasonably* generous measure) that not a vast volume of luncheon beverage wine (neither La Flora Blanche nor its stable-mate, Golden Guinea, but a modest, blameless little number from an obscure corner of the Loire) had been consumed before a thaw in the hitherto chilled atmosphere was distinctly perceptible; a marked degree of relaxation set in. Then, marvel of marvels, the two antagonists addressed each other – in terms of politeness, if not of warmth. I cannot imagine what professions of apology or explanation Christopher had managed to come up with, but the festivities finally ended with the two parties evincing an appearance of being on terms of mutual respect.

Many years later, that self-same *Good Food Guide* 'hit list' was to reverberate a little in my mind in quite a different way. The full roll of dishonour reads thus:

La Flora Blanche, Golden Guinea, Mateus Rosé, Liebfraumilch, Golden Oktober, Mouton Cadet, Chablis, Beaujolais,
Nuits Saint Georges and Châteauneuf-du-Pape (the generic
wines being suspect when offered without further identification).

This stern pronouncement on mass-market beverages was made, I
am sure, in the defence of individually made wines that are truly
representative of their regions (an attitude that I have every reason to
commend), but I thought then, and still feel now, that it was a rather
hard and sweeping judgement. Many has been the time when,
confronted by a dubious so-called wine list in, say, some provincial
Indian restaurant, I have bribed any of my children who happened to
be present to secrecy before ordering a bottle of . . . Mateus Rosé –
that appearing to be the least toxic beverage on offer – praying the
while that none of my customers should choose that moment to
partake of ethnic food.

When Tony Harrison (poet, playwright and noted classical scholar) generously provided some extremely freely adapted translations
of ancient Greek poems and aphorisms of vinous bent for the
adornment of a recent wine list. I was mildly concerned at this
English rendition of the cover verse:

Μενδαῖον, τοῦ μὲν καὶ ἐνουροῦσιν θεοί αὐτοί
στρώμασιν ἐν μαλακοῖς. Μάγνητα δὲ μειλιχόδωρον
καὶ Θάσιον, τῷ δὴ μήλων ἐπιδέδρομεν ὀδμή,
ταῦτον ἐγὼ κρίνω πολὺ πάντων εἶναι ἄριστον
τῶν ἄλλων οἴνων, μετ' ἀμύμονα Χῖον ἄλυπον.
ἔστι δέ τις οἶνος, τὸν δὴ σαπρίαν καλέουσιν,
οὗ καὶ ἀπὸ στόματος στάμνων ὑπανοιγομενάων
ὄζει ἴων, ὄζει δὲ ῥόδων, ὄζει δ' ὑακίνθου.
ὀσμὴ θεσπεσίη κατὰ πᾶν δ' ἔχει ὑψερεφὲς δῶ.
ἀμβροσία καὶ νέκταρ ὁμοῦ τοῦτ' ἐστὶ τὸ νέκταρ.
τούτου χρὴ παρέχειν πίνειν ἐν δαιτὶ θαλείῃ
τοῖσιν ἐμοῖσι φίλοις, τοῖς δ' ἐχθροῖς ἐκ Πεπαρήθου.

A Bourgeuil apostrophized as 'sheer
as taffeta' [good stocks at Mere!]
fragrant as violets dawn-wet with dew,
an apple-scented Closel from Anjou,
a Chinon L'Arpenty with 'hints of slate' –
such are the wines I keep to serve a mate!
[and all available from the Brothers Yapp!]
But none of the ones I've mentioned here
would I ever pour out for a man I hate.
People I can't stand entertaining, *they*
don't even get a modest *vin du pays*,
nor (neither *mousseux* nor *nature*) the Saint Péray
of the *vigneron* of Cornas, Auguste Clape
nor the '79 white Hermitage, Chante Alouette,
nor red, white, rosé Azay-le-Rideau
nor any château of the Loire, no, NO!
My enemies will be lucky if they get
[from some other merchants than the Brothers Yapp!]
served room-temperature, that *Liebfraulmilch* crap
or magnum after magnum of *Mateus Rosé!*

after Hermippus [fifth century BC]

My doubts were fully justified and rapidly realized; within a remarkably short space of time a letter of retribution arrived. Some kindly well-wisher had sped a copy of the list to Mr Fernando van Zeller Guedes, eighty-two-year-old chairman of Mateus Rosé, who wrote from Oporto to rap me over the knuckles (charmingly but most firmly) for what was, in his eyes, a dastardly act of *lèse-majesté*. Of course, I expressed abject contrition by the very next post, promising to be less of a 'closet consumer' of his famous product, and expressing the hope of one day being able to accept his kind invitation to visit him in Portugal so that I might pay homage at the very fountainhead of Mateus Rosé. Just what all this will do to my reputation and standing with the management of the *Good Food Guide*, I scarcely dare to imagine . . .

A Lamb to the Slaughter

The 'modest, blameless little number from an obscure corner of the Loire', the liberating libation that had ameliorated the potentially difficult atmosphere at my second London tasting, was a particularly pleasant (and pleasantly inexpensive) white wine that hailed from as obscure a corner of the Loire as might be found. Saint Pourçain-sur-Sioule is a small town on the banks of the rivers Allier and Sioule, sluggish streams that arise among the peaks of the Massif Central, and flow due north until joining the Loire as tributaries. Only a few kilometres from the spa town of Vichy, Saint Pourçain is virtually in the centre of France's huge landmass, and is a considerable distance away from any of the more usually acknowledged vineyards of the Loire. In a way, that white Saint Pourçain that was served under London Bridge Station symbolized something of a reason why my relationship with those cellars was becoming less close, and the way in which the nature of my business was increasingly swiftly beginning to alter.

As I gradually gained a little confidence (but, at the same time, and *far* more rapidly, realized what a horrendously enormous amount I had to learn), my collation of Rhône and Loire wines from other shippers' wholesale lists began to assume a complexion of parasitism, and grew less and less satisfying. I was well aware of my good fortune in having another profession – the emoluments of which helped to feed and clothe my family; this invaluable asset had meant that I could learn the hard way at least some of the commercial aspects of the business at fairly minimal risk, deduce the mechanics of shipping and of marketing, simultaneously trying to absorb all the myriad details of the backgrounds of my wares. To be absent from office and surgery was really problematic, but I had begun to make forays to the vineyards of Loire and Rhône whenever conceivably possible.

A sensible scheme, I reflected, would be to make the investigation of lesser, or quite frequently totally unknown, wines not already available in this country my strongest priority . . . so that is what I did.

The small town of Saint Pourçain-sur-Sioule was my first destination, its unassuming but agreeable wines my initial target. The town itself is rather dour in aspect, with only one or two attractive older buildings (the large tall-spired Gothic church in particular making up for the mediocrity of its neighbours) to mitigate the overall lack of architectural distinction or civic charm, as epitomized by the town's Michelin one-star restaurant and hotel, the Chêne Vert. For whatever else M. Michelin hands out his much sought-after rosettes, it is certainly not the elegance of the edifice of the establishment – or not in the case of the Chêne Vert, at any rate.

Once inside the hotel, matters were otherwise; it is a bustling family-run business, the culinary efforts of which (as I was later to discover) show exactly what M. Michelin esteems most. Having deposited my hold-all in the bedroom allotted me, I laboriously inquired as to the whereabouts of M. Pagnon's residence. It was extremely difficult to unravel the complexities of the *patronne's* highly involved directions and even more of a Herculean task to make any sense of the intricacies of a fiendishly baffling network of tortuous, unsignposted rural lanes.

When I wearily rolled into the object of my search's yard, I ruefully wished that I had not made the effort. M. Pagnon's family, his just-about *live*stock, his moth-eaten, bedraggled poultry, the least well-tended and most sprawling midden that I had ever beheld, even M. Pagnon himself, presented an ensemble that put me in mind of a run-down, miserable Cold Comfort Farm. Elie Pagnon, at the midriff level, might have been construed as a jolly Pickwickian fellow – by reason of rotund corpulence; his extremities, particularly the upper one, were far less reassuring. The close-set eyes that regarded me suspiciously, furtively looked me up and down from beneath a greasy flat cap (an adornment that appeared to be a permanent appendage), were distinctly shifty. In short, the figure that M. Elie Pagnon presented to the wide-open eyes of a stranger was less than prepossessing: I was in the presence of my very first real live French peasant, a rustic *vigneron*.

As always, there was that infernal language barrier to contend with, but this time the problem carried a slightly unusual aspect: it was highly debatable whether my shameful lack of French was in its way any worse than that of M. Pagnon, whose own version consisted of an unfathomable and incomprehensible patois delivered in hoarse gutturals. A grubby eleven-year-old lad was seconded to render his father's conversation into a fractionally more recognizable form of semi-standard French. Elie Pagnon could not have believed his luck, that squally afternoon in February: the very first foreigner to grace his hovel was quite patently as naïve as they ever came – in truth a lamb to the slaughter. M. Elie Pagnon began visibly to perk up, to smile an oily smile.

The method by which I had singled out this fortunate individual to be my first homespun supplier was, I had started out imagining, peculiarly fortuitous. A bottle of his white wine had been my chance selection in a village restaurant fifty kilometres away. As I had had no other prospective growers in mind, my feeling had been that the Fates must have wished to direct my footsteps – and, furthermore, the wine had been exceptionally potable. A brief inquiry of the mistress of the Chêne Vert had seemed to confirm that M. Pagnon might be my man.

That the grower had wine to sell was confirmed by some enthusiastic nodding; the urchin was dispatched post-haste to fetch a sample bottle. Beside us, working at an extremely battered table, an ill-favoured Mme Pagnon and other scruffy offspring were doing something most peculiar; they were making *porte-greffes* – grafting native vine plants on to American phylloxera-resistant root stock – although it took a year or so before I deduced that that must have been their chore. The wine was pronounced as sound by me, just as agreeable as at lunchtime – but any sense of trustful objectivity was fast being eroded by the dubiety of its birthplace. Just *how* could a blameless little wine like that emanate from such a sordid setting – a sort of down-market version of the L'il Abner strip cartoon community, but without the simple charm of the eponymous hero and absolutely lacking the pneumatic vivacity of a pretty Daisy Mae?

The fun began at this point; M. Pagnon really began to enjoy himself, while I began to feel very and ever increasingly 'green'; I simply had not the faintest idea what a justifiable and honest price might be. To be brutally frank, I knew nothing whatsoever about the purchase of wine in the field. The fact that I did not know how to or

care to haggle added such an unexpected dimension to the matter
that it threw my opponent for a moment, but that he felt recom-
pensed by the savage adverse differential I had so meekly and feebly
agreed to was demonstrated by the speed with which he regained his
stride.

Method of payment was the next item on the agenda. Cash up
front was the preference of the vendor; weakly, I agreed. When (while
pretending to check out the day's official rate in a tattered copy of the
Revue Agricole) M. Pagnon had creatively invented a, for him, highly
advantageous exchange rate, I was persuaded to produce my cheque
book, and to inscribe figures that he dictated, having first laboriously
scrawled columns of clumsy numerals on a page of a child's school
exercise book, produced by the eleven-year-old for that purpose. The
intense difficulty and tremendous responsibility that these arduous
calculations represented were evinced by the Frenchman's stentorian
breathing, and tongue stuck sideways out of mouth. M. Pagnon was
positively beaming as he snatched the still ink-wet cheque from my
hand; as he waved the piece of paper in the air to dry it, he suggested,
in crude dumb-show, that he would accompany me back to the
Chêne Vert, to help me through the difficulty of the lanes . . . and to
celebrate his amazing coup.

As I gradually calmed down after this extraordinary and bewildering sequence of events, and as I began to discern M. Pagnon's patent
and pleased air of self-congratulatory satisfaction, I tried to reconstruct, and to make sense of, the garbled succession of misadventures
which had comprised the afternoon's activities; I realized that I had
been taken for a formidable and comprehensive ride. My new chum,
Elie, beamed happily as he poured from the bottle of a further
example of my so-recent acquisition, a bottle that he had obtained
from an obliging Chêne Vert management at a price that was, I
noticed later at dinner, astonishingly similar to my own purchase
price – and I was already well aware that French restaurateurs
tended to think in terms of 300 per cent profit margins on their wines.

Gradually, in the days that followed, I was able to work out just
how extensively I had been exploited by the wily M. Pagnon. The
price had been outrageously extortionate, that indignity being
compounded by the inclusion of 'TVA' (we had not yet been impelled
into the nightmare mesh of value added tax in Britain, so I was not

even aware of the existence of such an impost) when export orders were specifically exempt from the French tax. The exchange rate he had so ingeniously concocted bore little, if any, resemblance to any official bank thinking then pertaining; it had been, naturally, heavily in the Frenchman's favour. Yet another reason that the sum demanded had been so astonishingly high was because the *vigneron* had thoughtfully elected to supply me with cases containing fifteen bottles, not the twelve that I had innocently envisaged.

When the full impact of M. Pagnon's devious manipulations had finally penetrated my skull, I astonished myself by the discovery of a hitherto unknown, latent entrepreneurial talent: I telephoned my bank in Gillingham with instructions to block payment of the cheque. This strikingly simple solution neatly reversed our roles, because a now presumably less than jubilant grower had put the twenty excessively heavy cartons into the hands of a forwarding agent, and could no longer call them back. The miscreant *did* receive his payment . . . in due course, at the then prevailing market exchange rate that had been calculated by someone reasonably competent in currency control.

On the principle that it is salutary to learn the worst at the earliest opportunity, I reckoned myself fortunate to have experienced and survived an encounter which proved to be the only such potential disaster of its kind. Now, if I had visted the Cordiers *first*, I would never have realized that French viticulture could have a seamy side.

Cordier Hospitality

After Saint Pourçain-sur-Sioule, Reuilly may be counted as the second most obscure corner of the Loire. I am not sure how it was that I had become aware of the little town's existence, let alone realized that the *commune* produced wine . . . and extremely good wine it turned out to be – when I finally got to sample it. Fifteen kilometres west of the lovely provincial capital of Berry, Bourges (with an outstandingly beautiful cathedral, the magnificent fourteenth-century stained glass windows of which rival those of Chartres itself), Reuilly is the very epitome of a small French market town. Unfortunately, the Cordier family had chosen to spend the past few centuries at La Ferté, a tiny rustic hamlet two kilometres south along the road to Issoudun.

As most of their sales were made to individual clients, who called to collect their purchases, Aimée, Mme Cordier, was not all that surprised to receive a visitor but, as her very first Englishman, I caused something of a stir. When she had composed herself, after such a novel event, her welcome was enormous. Preoccupied with alchemical stirrings at a huge black stove, she ushered me into the cottage's kitchen – the heart, hearth and pivot of the place – and sat me at the table. Leaving me with a black-clad granny, who sat silently in a corner by the fire, Mme Cordier crossed the yard to look for her husband in the barn.

The whole bucolic establishment had a peaceful, reassuring air; the rich smell of good food hung in the air. The cottage was last in a little terrace of three: as the generations had passed, so another dwelling had been added – for the habitation of a son or a daughter (at my next visit to La Ferté, the challenge of finding the place was rendered the more confusing because a fourth cottage had been added in the interval – a house for the Cordier son, Gérard, and his very recent bride). A courtyard was encircled by a mixture of outbuildings and a large, plain but imposing stone barn. I was soon to learn that the family's cellar lay beneath that massive barn.

A cheerily smiling M. Cordier came striding across the yard, followed by his equally cheerful little wife, whose plump, apple-red cheeks and radiantly merry grin irresistibly put me in mind of an idealized farmer's wife from a book of children's tales, or of the perfect Mrs Noah. Very sensibly, she had gone in search of her husband with an empty pitcher in hand. This she now brought into the kitchen, brimful of translucent Reuilly wine. As Aimée poured out what proved to be an exceptionally delicious wine, Robert began to tell me about the *appellation*, and of how he made his wine.

Theirs was a *polyculture*, a little of everything; a hectare or so of arable land was used to cultivate sweet corn, *maïs* – as was evidenced by a weird contraption, constructed from timbers and wire netting, in a corner of the yard: this towering rack was filled to the brim with countless cobs of corn, destined to feed five cows – a further aspect of the family's economy. Viticulture, the main part of the Cordiers' hard-working life, was made far more arduous by the complicated division of their pieces of land. The French system of inheritance is not one of primogeniture, as used to be the case in Britain, where the eldest son normally inherited the whole estate. Traditionally, in France and here, in Reuilly, as each generation succeeded, any land owned by the family had for centuries been divided among surviving siblings. By this time, the Cordiers' seven hectares of vineyard were scattered randomly through the parish, varying enormously in size – from two hectares down to the odd half-row of vines. (It is of interest to note that each proprietor always knows *exactly* where in a row his vines commence, and precisely which are his neighbours', without recourse to the official definitive plan lodged in the archives of the *mairie*.) By the nature of these historic subdivisions, an uncomfortably large proportion of the daily workload consisted of simply moving themselves and implements around the *appellation*.

By this time, son Gérard had returned from the fields in hopeful anticipation of a midday meal – the tantalizing aromas of which were permeating the cottage. The presence of an outlandish stranger disturbed him not a jot; he poured himself a glass of wine (which by now had transmuted itself into a delicate, pale-coral rosé) – Robert having made several visits to the cellar across the yard to replenish the empty jug. Quietly nodding in my direction, Gérard took his place at the table. His mother put out some cutlery, and unhesitatingly laid a knife and fork in front of me – the knife was an effete luxury to help out an ill-prepared visitor: Robert and Gérard fished out formidable clasp-knives from the recesses of their blue overalls, opened out the cut-throat blades, and proceeded to hack a huge round country loaf, the size of a millstone, into man-sized hunks of bread.

The still incommunicative grandmother was aided to her place at table, while my hostess ladled out vast volumes of aromatic onion soup from a fire-blackened *marmite* that took up half the surface of the stove. A platter of assorted *charcuterie* followed fast – *jambon cru*, sausages of various types, and a really delicious pâté which, when I finally managed to look up *grive* in my little blue Collins French-English dictionary, disconcertingly turned out to be made from thrush! As usual, the greatest impediment to an exceptionally happy occasion was my hopeless lack of French; my ineptitude must surely have strained the patience of these good folk: every other word had to be prised from the pages of that much-thumbed dictionary. But, somehow, communication *did* prove possible; indeed, my fluency seemed to improve dramatically as the pitcher made further voyages across the yard.

I was even able to comprehend that I was expected to take *my* turn at refilling the jug; the minuscule underground chamber, grandly called the 'cellar', that lay beneath the barn housed half a dozen time-worn wooden barrels, *tonneaux*, containing the original delicious white Reuilly, product of the Sauvignon grape; the finely nuanced rosé, made from Pinot Gris; or a robust, earthy Gamay red. The butler of the moment enjoyed the privilege of selecting the colour of the wine.

My choice had fallen on the rosé, when what I had assumed to be a nearly completed meal resurged into activity with the production from the capacious oven of a pungent, garlic-impregnated chicken – no water-impregnated supermarket fowl *this* magnificent beast, but a veritable *poulet de Bresse*: the sort of *poulet* that comes with an official birth certificate, a document guaranteeing the animal's pedigree and giving assurance of an intensive diet of maize. A straightforward but deeply satisfying *gratin savoyarde* (thinly sliced potatoes that had been simmered for hours and hours in a tasty broth of stock) and an equally uncomplicated salad of *mâche sauvage*, lamb's lettuce, garnered that morning from between the rows of vines, lightly tossed in a *vinaigrette* based upon an appetizing, locally made walnut oil.

Any residual shyness on my part totally evaporated as we shared this gorgeous feast . . . *and* as the wine continued to flow. As we toyed with several local cheeses, I tentatively and diffidently inquired about the possibility of making a modest purchase of the lovely wines. The entire family (with the exception of the old lady) fairly laughed their heads off at the very idea of such a ridiculous suggestion – albeit as kindly as they could. With an annual production of a mere several hundred cases, and with an eager and intensely loyal local clientele, there was simply no wine at all to spare. When I eventually made my departure, these generously hospitable people urged me to return to La Ferté the next time that I might find myself in the vicinity. As I turned the car towards the gate, Robert made a sudden dash to one of the stone buildings, and returned just as swiftly, brandishing a couple of bottles of his precious white wine, which he presented to me as a souvenir of as memorably happy a first encounter as I had ever experienced . . . but there would be no commercial shipment of Reuilly to Britain – for that year, at least.

The following spring, I made my way to Reuilly, and eventually found the now augmented Cordier house. That I was fully expected to share the copious family luncheon was not in question. The same delightful routine ensued, varied only by the arrival of Gérard's bride of recent date from her job in Reuilly, to add to the conviviality. As the afternoon progressed, it became apparent that the Cordiers had held family councils during the intervening months; with an air of some solemnity, as we addressed ourselves to home-made *eau-de-vie de poire William*, Robert cleared his throat to make an important announcement: if I were still to wish it, twenty-five cases of the family's delicious product would be allocated to my use.

Nowadays, many visits later, Britain is so fortunate as to receive a little more than half the Cordiers' yearly harvest. I try not to let my thoughts dwell on what might have become of their erstwhile local clients, or as to where they now must forage to keep their cellars full.

The annual luncheon at La Ferté is a highlight of my travels through the Loire though, upon occasion, the atmosphere has been less than truly festive. Twelve years ago my then seven-year-old son came with me as companion on a trip to Rhône and Loire. When we arrived at the Cordiers' cottage, it was plain that all was far from well. Robert's elder brother and sister-in-law were present; the solemn air of everyone, and the men's black ties and unaccustomed suits, indicated the reason for the prevailing gloom: the family had just returned from the interment of the grandmother at Reuilly's cemetery. Even bereavement had failed to distract Aimée's devotion to her stove: the funeral feast was excellent, the non-stop passage of the wine jugs to and fro just as relentless as any other year. Jason was far too young to notice or to realize the situation; it was his childish prattle *and* the lovely Cordier wine that together served to lift the ambient gloom.

The following year was easier and, as it turned out, constituted a celebration. The arranged date for our reunion happened to fall upon my birthday: a coincidence that I must have casually let slip. The conversation was lively (for, by now, my French was rather more communicative) and I failed to observe that Gérard's pretty wife, Isabelle, had slipped away to Reuilly. Gradually, it dawned upon me that something out of ordinary seemed to be going on; the peculiarity mainly lying in an unusual dilatoriness in the preparation of food. Still, the wine gushed as though from a magical, limitless spring, and an animated exchange of information fully occupied the time. Then a most remarkable thing happened: a broadly smiling Aimée led me to a door leading from the kitchen. For the very first time, I realized that the house boasted a dining room, a luxury hitherto unrevealed to me. An extensive table had been rendered admirably festive with candles and pretty flowers – and a full complement of cutlery. While I had been being distracted, a full, magnificent birthday feast had been in course of rapid preparation! On this auspicious occasion, Robert and Gérard were (with reluctance) prepared to dispense with the assistance of their favourite clasp-knives, to add significance to the party by the use of normal household knives.

And what a spread it was! It should be to our national gastronomic shame that we could not possibly create a similar instant culinary performance. In which small rural town in England might one hope to procure ten dozen succulent oysters on a Tuesday, at midday? Certainly not Gillingham or Mere. In England, one might go from one year to the next without clapping eyes on a *langouste*, but Reuilly had provided three splendid specimens which were incomparably delightful in their lightly grilled perfection, as they lay before us on our plates. Fresh asparagus followed shellfish: simple, but delicious in a straightforward butter sauce. A quartet of fine oven-bronzed, crisp-skinned Barbary ducks, surrounded by mounds of equally brown, carefully sculpted roast potatoes, gave adequate excuse to move on to the red wine of the house. A much needed pause to the proceedings was provided by a refreshing *frisée* salad.

The habitual three or four regional cheeses had been augmented threefold for this day; the close-crammed cheeseboard would even have gladdened the eyes of Major Patrick Rance of Streatley! A towering pyramid of black-chocolate-drenched profiteroles constituted the pudding . . . but by then I was incontrovertibly over-satiated, so I toyed with a fluteful of its accompanying champagne instead. The standard, inevitable, home-distilled *eau-de-vie de poire William* was a genuinely needed *digestif* – something as flavoursomely potent was definitely needed to kick-start the gastric demolition of my suffering stomach's contents.

For a number of years, I had begun to be aware of mounting Cordier pressure for me to time my call for Easter, so that is what I did one year. Judith and I elected to billet ourselves at Reuilly's only hotel, the Prieuré – itself a bizarre enough establishment, a detailed description of which would merit a chapter of its own (there *was* another hotel down by the railway station – where Bokassa had once stayed, but local opinion firmly believed that the attractive chambermaids never left the bedrooms, so my wife had turned *that* particular option down). An ancient building, the Prieuré had indeed been ecclesiastical in origin, and was semi-detached from Reuilly's medieval church. The sad oddity of the place chiefly lay in the fact that its *patronne*, who had once been a successful mannequin, was now a raving alcoholic who could no longer be trusted in the employment of her gleaming battery of copper casseroles, and who passed her time in really serious appraisal of the merits or demerits of the local wine.

Multicoloured bunting festooned the streets and square, and indicated that something special was about to happen. Over oysters in their kitchen that Good Friday evening, Robert and Aimée finally revealed the truth: Easter marked the moment of an annual wine fair; the *foire aux vins* constituted the small town's principal festivity each year.

When we looked out upon the square from our Prieuré bedroom window the next morning, the small *place* had been transformed during the night. The usual ranks of parked cars had been replaced by peripheral rows of neat canvas booths, each four-square stall carrying a sign proclaiming the name of a local *vigneron*; a grander erection taking up a central position announced itself as head-quarters of the oyster vendors of Chaillevette, a fishing village on the Atlantic coast which had somehow established a particular relation-ship with Reuilly over the years, and sent an oyster-laden contingent of citizens to every Reuilly communal event – an ideal affinity, as Reuilly's white wine matched the plump Chaillevette oysters to perfection.

Tucked in the shadow of the church's flying buttresses stood a most amazing and exceedingly colourful phenomenon which, upon close examination, proved to be a travelling dance hall which had made countless annual visits to the villages of Berry for half a century or more. Now surely meriting a preservation order at the hands of the *beaux-arts*, this exotic building was outrageously art deco, with 'sunburst' fenestration and a framework creatively coloured in extraordinary hues. Although no one knew it, that was to be the Printanier's (for it boasted its own name) last visit to Reuilly: a new, unpopular and highly officious *curé* took exception to the otherwise inoffensive *bal musette ambulant*'s nocturnal noise so close to the church, and succeeded in achieving a total ban. The Printanier comes no more to Reuilly; the town's *salle des réunions* is in no way an adequate substitute.

By 11 a.m. the striped awnings of the wine booths had been unfurled, and serious-faced growers began to arrange their wares. The little knots of townsfolk, who had by now started to assemble in large numbers at the approaches to the *place*, looked eagerly expec-tant as the strains of discordant bagpipe music came floating down the street. A small but very solemn procession then came into view, slowly progressing down the main street, from *mairie* to *foire*, preceded by the bagpiper. The mayor escorted that most important personage, the *député* of the region, with a cluster of other stiff-suited dignitaries closely in attendance. As president of Reuilly's *viticulteurs*, Robert Cordier walked in the vanguard of this curious cohort of provincial personalities.

The temporary entrance to the *place* comprised a towering wooden archway, with large wooden cut-out letters suspended across its pediment spelling out *FOIRE AUX VINS* in most impressive style. As the procession came to a halt at the archway, a small girl was pushed out of the awaiting throng by an anxious *maman*; proffering a pair of scissors to the august figure of the *député*, the child made a pretty curtsy, and fled back to her mother as quickly as she had emerged. His cutting of a symbolic red ribbon stretched tautly between the entrance's upright posts was the signal for a further painful air upon the bagpipes, some rather inaccurately rendered fanfares from a pair of hunting horns . . . and, *of course*, the speeches: absolutely *de rigueur* at *all* French civic occasions. I am ashamed to have to confess that my otherwise most worthy friend, Robert's, oration was no less lengthy than that of the *député* . . . or the *maire*, or those of the three other dignitaries who were not prepared to forgo an opportunity of making maximum use of a public address system (which was so defective as to render all the harangues utterly unintelligible – even to the bystanding Frenchmen).

At blessed, peaceful last, everyone who imagined he was anyone had had his final say. Then the official party, headed by the *député*, made a stately circuit of the twenty or thirty stalls; an obligatory small glass of Reuilly was solemnly imbibed by each member of the entourage at every single stand. Their samples were free – we common folk had to hand over a few centimes for our glasses of wine, as we followed in the politicians' footsteps. The Cordiers' kiosk occupied a place of honour, last in the line-up, right next to the Printanier. A visibly perspiring (and unaccustomedly suited) Gérard was assisted by his mother in the hectic task of dispensing specimens to the urgently demanding mêlée. When the mob of eager *dégustateurs* had dispersed a little, we were able to engage in a more thoughtful reappraisal of the delicious Cordier wine.

We were still engaged in this delightfully serious responsibility, when the stallholders began to shutter their stands. Robert, who had by now come to have a chat, indicated that we should follow him . . . into the Printanier. We passed half a dozen Chaillevettoise, who were feverishly opening oysters, as we entered the main hall of the historic *bal musette*. Tables and chairs for upwards of two hundred people had been arranged across the dance floor for a most munificent feast; a scramble for seats was in progress, but Gérard and Isabelle had already secured places for our party, next to a group of young gendarmes. As Judith joined the youngsters, Robert plucked my sleeve and led me to a supposed place of honour, near him on the top table.

That banquet was a further staggering example of just how superbly organized the French can be . . . when it comes to food. The strenuous efforts of the Chaillevette oyster operatives started the proceedings – a dozen succulent oysters each – to stimulate the gastric juices; *pâté de foie gras* to follow, and no namby-pamby, penny-pinching portions either – man-sized blocks of rich goose liver were liberally handed out; salmon steaks were bathed in pools of pungent *beurre blanc*: a most substantial fish course. As any Englishman would have done in my position, I assumed that the truffle-studded guinea fowl served *en croûte* with butter-softened salsify represented the apogee of that formidable banquet – but my supposition was incorrect: that honour fell to vast pieces of tender Charollais beef (so mouth-watering was its tenderness that its rareness – still virtually throbbing – for once failed to appal me) and towering mounds of fine-cut, well-salted *pommes frites*.

As the long afternoon pursued its languid course, as dish succeeded dish, I rather began to resent Judith's good fortune in being part of an animated circle of younger people at the far end of one of the long communal tables. My neighbours were respectable minor local government officials; any topics of remotely mutual interest had been exhausted an hour or so before; I had ample opportunity to observe that the pace had been too gruelling for the ninety-year-old *député*: he had fallen asleep, chin on chest, in the seat of honour. The only compensation for the social limitations of where I had been placed was that we of the top table were being liberally satiated with rather better wines than were the hoi-polloi below, but I noticed that, even there, Gérard had taken the sensible precaution of stashing a dozen bottles of his father's best *cuve* beneath his seat.

Cheese was easy – a choice of only seven – but an over-solicitous waitress insisted on putting a generous wedge of each upon my plate. The puddings I would prefer to forget: they were copious and rich. By the time that small cups of strong black coffee arrived (accompanied by a startlingly numerous selection of marcs and eaux-de-vie, dusk was falling . . . and I could scarcely stir.

The waitresses made it obvious that they were anxious for our departure, so that they might rearrange the hall. Earlier in the day, Gérard had introduced me to my professional counterpart, Reuilly's sole dental surgeon – *also* a wine enthusiast. My new-found Gallic colleague positively insisted that I should join him in a visit to his surgery, several streets away. Leaving my wife safely in the Cordiers' hands, Claude and I wove a little unsteadily across the cobblestones of the square, to view his impressive premises in a charming seventeenth-century courtyard. When I had vociferously admired his new equipment, Claude swayed across the room towards a drugs cabinet mounted on the wall. It transpired that, in Reuilly, patients' dental crises were occasionally assuaged by the administration of forty-year-old Armagnac – a sovereign remedy for toothache that struck me, in our present emergency, as being a marvellous scheme. With mouthwash tumblers safely in our hands, Claude proposed a toast to the continuance of the *entente cordiale* from the recesses of an armchair, to which I responded as gracefully as I could from my semi-recumbent position on the electrically operated dental chair.

Judith and the Cordiers had been on the point of sending out a search party (assisted by Armagnac-barrelled St Bernards?) when my new friend and I finally reappeared at the travelling *salle de danse*. Much purposeful activity was in progress there, a vigorous repositioning of the fold-up chairs (the trestle tables were already back in storage, against another year). My friends gently seated me at the aisle end of a row of chairs somewhere near a freshly erected dais, Judith gently patting my hand, Aimée, Gérard and Isabelle further along the row.

With astonishing rapidity, the hall was packed with people – many having to stand at the rear of the dance floor. The peaceful hubbub of conversation was rudely pierced by a cacophony of trumpet fanfares, as a strangely garbed company slowly progressed up the aisle: a *chapitre* of the Maîtrise des Echansons de Reuilly en Berry had just commenced its proceedings on that evening of 17 April 1976. The participating *vignerons* looked very different from their usual vineyard work-clad selves, in the supposedly medieval robes that their wives or girlfriends had lovingly stitched together.

As *grand maître*, a completely transformed Robert Cordier declared the *chapitre* to be in session, in a form of Middle French. The object of the exercise, an amusing and appealing form of public relations, was to elect into the brotherhood various Reuilly-related personalities of the region. One after another, the candidates went forward, and on to the stage: the editor of the local agricultural newspaper, a recently appointed *chef* of the town's *gendarmerie*, a much esteemed agricultural engineer, and so on, to swear fealty to Reuilly – specifically the wine in this instance – and to join the *confrérie*.

Some discontent among the town's people began to manifest itself: the postulants were *not* performing well. One of the most important parts of the ceremony was supposed to be the *renversement* of the entire contents of a bottle of Reuilly into an enormous goblet; amazingly enough, the participants seemed to balk at what ought to have been a simple enough task . . . perhaps they had been made aware of the next part of the rite: *theoretically*, an ideal new entrant into the Maîtrise should, when prompted, drain the massive vessel in one draught, as a compliment to the wine. One after the other, the Frenchmen failed miserably to perform the required chore, muttering vaguely about problems with their *foies*. At no time did the level in the glass approach even the halfway mark; the audience was *not* happy with this unexpected turn of events.

Suddenly Judith nudged me into a state of full alertness; the *confrérie*'s master of ceremonies was calling out an approximation of my name! With more than a little momentary confusion, I mounted the rostrum; aware of an awesome responsibility as an unfortunate representative of Britain, I turned to face the hostile crowd. When I had haltingly taken the oath, the moment for *renversement* arrived; Robert, clad in embroidered velvet and brocade, handed me the bottle which, I was thankful to note, was his home brew. He nodded at me vigorously when the moment came to pour. That anything less than transferring every last drop from bottle to goblet would suffice was irresistibly indicated by Robert's stern mien, when it momentarily appeared that I might do less than full justice to the 75 cl that the bottle claimed to hold. I poured the lot.

Though somewhat bemused (as well I might be, after the rigours of the day), when I slowly and with difficulty raised that absurdly heavy chalice to my far from thirsty lips, it clearly dawned upon my fuddled senses that, as the first stranger ever to be so honoured in this hospitable community, a fearsome obligation lay upon my reluctant shoulders – or reluctant gullet, as it were. Addressing my attention to the limpid ocean that sparkled in the enormous stoup, I drew a mighty breath, and then, deliberately and purposefully, drained every single drop . . . without pausing for breath.

The populace of the Printanier went crazy – the only standing ovation that I am ever likely to receive; I am almost prepared to aver that hats went sailing through the air. When the hubbub eventually subsided, and people had been persuaded to return to their places, Robert gave me a smile, and an approving nod and wink. Gingerly descending from the dais, I returned to my seat, being back-slapped on my way by vociferous well-wishers.

The last remaining aspirant for the glory of *intronisation* into the Maîtrise was a large man, a restaurateur from nearby Châteauroux – a front row forward by the look. This giant of a fellow had no hesitation in following my example; he smoothly consumed his bottle's worth of Reuilly's lovely product – which greatly pleased the crowd.

The evening's formal festivities now being at an end, the burly M. Jean Bardet came over to hug me, practically lifting me into the air in the painful process. Back on my own two feet, I regretfully had to decline his excellent suggestion that we should make a circuit of all the bars of Reuilly together – a sort of triumphant two-man rugby tour – because I had already accepted an invitation to an oyster feast *chez* Cordier; all I had time for was a stomach-settling Löwenbrau together in the bar of the neighbouring Prieuré, before driving out to La Ferté for a confrontation with dozens and dozens of Chaillevette oysters . . . and *lots* more delicious Reuilly. Now that my old mate, Jean, has acquired a third Michelin rosette for his eating-house in Châteauroux, it occurs to me that it might be agreeable to look him up on my next trip through the Loire.

The weekend's revels concluded on the Sunday with a carnival cavalcade, a colourful procession which the whole district turned out to see. The *mairie* was the starting point, and it was the important incumbent of that office who was to signal the moment when the Reuilly brass band should commence to play. As he was about to do so, the *maire* happened to glimpse me in the crowd. When he beckoned in my direction, good-natured bystanders cheerfully propelled me towards the steps upon which the dignitary stood. Shaking me warmly by the hand, the hirsute mayor proceeded to give me a whiskery, garlicky kiss upon each cheek, and launched into a short impromptu speech that (I was later told) made flattering reference to Britain's potential capacity to absorb all the wine of France – but Reuilly in particular. Only then was the parade allowed to begin its annual triumphant tour.

Various Visitors

Back in Wiltshire, at Hinckes Mill House, matters were progressing – though in a somewhat haphazard fashion. My storage arrangements for wine were exceedingly, painfully, simple; an initial jumble of Lichine-marked boxes towards the rear of the garage floor just about permitted the garaging of a car. This lack of system was succeeded by flimsy Dexion shelves which carried cardboard wine cartons placed on their sides. Small numbered tickets were supposed to convey the impression that these insubstantial makeshift containers represented wine bins. The surplus cases of wine, some bearing the names of well-known London shippers, remained as a jumble on the floor: never again was there an opportunity to use the garage for its intended purpose – to house a car.

The extreme rusticity of those *ad hoc* arrangments embarrassed me considerably when callers knocked upon the door – which was becoming an increasingly frequent occurrence. For a long time, it seemed that it was virtually axiomatic that the type of person who combined a consuming passion for esoteric wines with the heroic persistence needed actually to find the place, chose and had the funds to travel in very exotic cars.

The first such visitor was walking down the lane with two enormous Old English sheepdogs when I returned from my surgery one lunchtime; his rugged looks and the expensive simplicity of his country clothes made Peter Wood, already famous as a theatre director, look distinctly out of place in a muddy Wiltshire lane. When I came to a halt before the house, a soft-top crimson only-available-on-the-Continent Porsche Targa already parked there seemed fantastically outlandish – especially in comparison to my battered, cow dung-spattered vehicle.

With great charm and tact, Peter appeared to fail to notice the inadequacies of my so-called cellar, choosing instead to address himself with enthusiasm to the bottle of Muscadet that I plied him with in the conservatory. An hour or so later, when he had successfully crammed two cases of wine, the two large dogs *and* himself into the beautiful but diminutive Targa, we cheerfully exchanged waves and smiles of farewell.

It was several months before I learned that, in a valiant (and successful) attempt to avoid hitting my farmer neighbour's miserable cur, my recent client had lost control of his lovely mode of transport upon the slippery surface of the mudpan that called itself a lane. Unfortunately, the Porsche caused far more damage to itself than to the stone parapets of the bridge over the river Stour at the bottom of the hill, and had to be repatriated to Germany for ferociously costly repairs. Whether the incident gave him an aversion to Yapp Muscadet, or whether he temporarily could not afford to, it was the best part of a year before Peter returned to buy more wine.

Some months later, a handsome Rolls-Royce surfaced in my life. Business over for the week, I was quietly entertaining local friends at a simple Saturday family luncheon in the kitchen when an insistent pealing of the door bell made me leave my social duties. An uncommonly smart person stood upon the door mat. Having negotiated the tiny roads in an enormous limousine, my unheralded visitor categorically refused my half-hearted attempt to plead that I was shut: he insisted upon attention. Very reluctantly, having explained the situation, I installed him in the sitting room with a copy of the list . . . *and* a bottle of Muscadet – for that wine was the pretext for his call.

When I was able to return from carving activities fifteen minutes later, the desire to purchase a dozen bottles of Muscadet seemed to have completely slipped away. The pinstriped potential customer was in a state of great excitement; fascinated by the columns of unfamiliar and unknown names in the catalogue, he now urgently demanded to buy a specimen bottle of absolutely everything in the list.

As I pulled each bottle from its tatty cardboard compartment, my chagrin mounted at the thought of being proprietor of such shabby, homely arrangements; as I handed down the wines, to make up mixed case after assorted case – fourteen in all – and as I carefully placed each case in the boot of the immaculate Rolls-Royce, I felt more and more embarrassed. To my great astonishment, the unexpected visitor seemed to be even more elated than before – in fact, he was fairly hugging himself with glee. At this point, he introduced himself; at the age of thirty-eight, Nicholas Ryman had only recently divested himself (and advantageously too) of his family's stationery business. The vast contrast between what had been until so recently *his* nationwide empire, with hundreds of employees and all the appurtenances of big business, and *my* humble one-man band appealed to Nick enormously. To see an enterprise at its outset was, he said, most attractive; within a short space of time he envisaged me employing helpers – among other things, to drive a fleet of fork-lift trucks. I laughed . . . albeit *most* politely.

Nick returned to Hinckes Mill House within a fortnight, choosing to arrive in a splendid dark-blue Dino Ferrari – instead of a previously threatened helicopter. His mission was to proposition me; with many a plausible argument and with impeccably reasoned logic my new acquaintance urged upon me the wisdom of allowing him to invest massively (by my most modest standards) in my embryonic, half-baked business, to install me in an emporium in London anywhere that I might care to name – even Tooley Street, if so desired.

Just how I managed to resist those truly tempting blandishments I really cannot now imagine – other than that I was only too very well aware of how pathetically little I knew about my recently chosen *métier*, from background information about the wines' sources to concepts of how to market the stuff, and of business methods and commercial management. Eventually, several meetings later, Nick lost patience with me, and accepted my fervently grateful refusal; he bought a pretty wine estate near Bergerac, and went to live in France. With much patience, immense attention to detail and a great deal of unremitting faith, he has made the vineyards of Château la Jaubertie into one of the most successful and admired estates to be found anywhere outside the historically famous viticultural regions of France. I felt almost rueful as I watched him pack up to emigrate; there were going to be many moments in subsequent years when I wished that Nick, or someone very much like him, would appear upon my doorstep . . . to make a similar financial offer!

I cannot remember what type of limousine the man from Richmond favoured, except that it was black, clean (something of a rarity in our parts) and smart enough to impress me. But I was already convinced of Mr Smith's status in the fashionable world: he was the first potential customer who, having received my list through the post, had telephoned to arrange a meeting with me at Hinckes Mill House. Most precise, was Mr Smith; he could drive from Richmond on the agreed day; his quest was for a light dessert wine – perhaps something delicious from the Loire? – a not *too* sweetish wine, where the sugar might be counterbalanced by a refreshing residual acidity: in short, the ideal wine with which to partner fresh raspberries and cream.

Having cleared the refrigerator of boring utilities like butter, milk and Indian tonic water, I carefully arranged in it a bottle of each of the wines I then stocked that might fit the bill – seven wines in all. My visitor was as precise in his arrival as in his arrangements (I had sent a sketch map to help him through the lanes) but, somewhat to my surprise, drove himself – no chauffeur anywhere in sight.

Speaking platitudes of welcome, I ushered my distinguished customer (he did look *extremely* respectable) into the sitting room. No sooner seated than up he bounded again: he had left a most important briefcase in the car. While Mr Smith retrieved his luggage, I busied myself with collecting bottles from the fridge. As I drew seven corks, he opened up the black leather valise, and abstracted three plastic containers and a bowl: to my open-mouthed astonishment, Mr Smith proceeded to pour raspberries from the first, and cream from the next carton (the third contained caster sugar). At this point, it was discovered that an essential spoon had been omitted from the case. Under the circumstances, I could do nothing less than search out one of the children's christening spoons – that the instrument should be silver was clearly axiomatic.

With the utmost solemnity, Mr Smith tasted each of the seven glasses set before him, the various examples of Coteaux du Layon, Chaume, even a Quarts de Chaume *and* a Bonnezeaux! Slowly, the raspberries disappeared – without my being offered a single one – as he bobbed among the glasses, sipping first this one, then that, and back again. Forty minutes later, my guest appeared to have reached a decision of some import; nodding his head in guarded approval, he indicated that one of my offerings had survived the ordeal by raspberry.

Before nominating the successful candidate, delivery must be discussed. Like so many Londoners, he explained, his apartment in Richmond lacked adequate cellaring space. However, he was fortunate in having established particularly cordial relations with the wine buyer at the Army and Navy Stores in Victoria Street: the cellarman there was prepared to store Mr Smith's wine purchases on a long-term basis. He checked and double-checked that I had got the instructions clearly and firmly in my head: indeed, I wrote them down in minute detail, and he verified that I had got them right. On such and such a day, at such a time, the wine now under question would be put into the capable hands of the cellarman at the Army and Navy Stores. Agreed? Agreed.

Then Mr Smith revealed his big decision: it was the most modest of the array that had taken his particular fancy, a simple, pleasant Vouvray rejoicing in the name of 'Valentine', a product of a *négociant* house at Saint Hilaire-Saint Florent, near Saumur, at the princely cost of 13s 6d a bottle; would I see to it that four bottles of this Vouvray arrived punctually in Victoria Street?

Very gradually, business began to pick up, sales to increase; the five cases of wine sold each week in the course of the first year built up to thirty, then more, as time went by. My able personal assistant, Miss Felicity Maw-Forbes, had gone on to foreign parts, but I was just about managing to walk the perilous tightrope of running two utterly disparate and quite demanding enterprises – an unusual 'double act' that continued for sixteen years in all; naturally, the hours of work were considerable (to say the least!), but life was tremendous fun. And all the while, the good and beneficient Cyril Ray was quietly continuing his inestimable efforts on my behalf.

An invitation to pass a weekend at Cyril and Elizabeth Ray's splendid house in Kent was, of course, irresistible. However, my arrival was not without mishap: my car definitively and expensively broke down fifty miles from Delmonden Manor. When I had come to terms with abandoning the contraption by the roadside, and finally managed a much delayed landfall by taxi, my hosts were charmingly forgiving; Ray calmed me with injections of pink champagne while Liz resurrected an oven-bound dinner. After a refreshing and restorative supper, I was introduced to something that has been a much appreciated friend ever since: Taylor's Twenty Years Old Tawny Port.

Ray has never been particularly interested in port (though it would be quite unsafe to leave an unpadlocked bottle of good cognac *anywhere* in his vicinity), so he elected me his representative in investigating the comparative virtues of Messrs Taylor, Fladgate and Yeatman's stunning range of tawny ports. I quickly warmed to this interesting, responsible task, and very soon got the hang of things; back and forth I went, tasting and reassessing the Ten Years, the Twenty and the subtle, delicious Forty Years Old Tawnies. I am now prepared to admit that I continued that arduous labour for rather longer than was *strictly* necessary, because I had given the supreme accolade to the Twenty Years at a relatively early stage in the proceedings, but I thought it prudent to double- and treble-check for my host's journalistic reputation. It was a decision that I have never had cause to regret over what now adds up to many years of intermittent, but always considered, research . . . and *that* was the wine that was singled out as having particular merit in Mr Ray's next *Observer* wine article.

Our next adventure together was in the Loire Valley the following summer. The Rays were chairpersons of an eminently respectable wine society, and that year's venue for a society outing happened to be the Loire. Would I, in my capacity as a *supposed* authority on that valley's marvellous product, join the party in the vineyards, and give its members the benefit of my infinite knowledge on the subject? I could hardly refuse, but I was in poor condition when I finally found the group.

Any possible benefits of a family holiday spent in the south-west of France had been eroded to the point of extinction by a five-hour delay (due to gross overbooking) in a sandwich-less, but pastis-plenteous airport bar in Montpellier, a half-hour turn round at home before dashing off to man a wine stand at a trade fair in London, another half-hour in which to repack a case, before a night ferry to Le Havre which gave very little beneficial repose. Breaking journey records, I felt fairly self-satisfied when I staggered into the Hôtel Royal on the avenue Grammont in Tours. My belief that our assignation was to have been here, at base, was mistaken, I learned, with stupefied consternation. Monsieur Ray's *petit cercle* should by then, be in

Chambord. I was instantly presented with a glass of local wine by an ever-attentive Ray when I crept into a wistaria-clad *auberge* next to the tourist car park. Such had been my ordeal by hours of sleeplessness and overlong kilometres that I had to ask Ray to place the brimfull glass on the table before me so that I could lean forward to siphon up a modicum: I dared not trust my shaking hands. It was really quite effective, that simple drop of Cheverny; when my untouched dessert had been taken away, I was just about able to deliver an oration on the indisputable splendours of the wines of the Loire.

Two days later, official duties over, just a nucleus of the Ray's particular chums remained in situ at the Royal. We who breakfasted early rejoiced to see the sun. Reggie Peck, an old journalist friend of Ray's, who took his *petit déjeuner* in the hotel's bar in the form of bottled beer, glowered morosely at the unexpected beams of light falling across the floor. Somehow, a sudden decision was taken to put together a picnic and make an excursion to the countryside. Liz and Esmé, the other female of our vestigial band of five (who turned out to be, I was most impressed to learn, the Dowager Countess of Carlisle), volunteered to rustle up some food from a nearby *alimentation* if I would undertake to organize the wine. Reggie and Ray were dispatched to forage for toothmugs from our hotel rooms.

Trying to air my local knowledge, I directed us west of Tours, on the southern bank of the Loire; by dint of some excellent map reading by Esmé, we crossed the river Indre at Ponts de Ruan, where remnants of what used in Balzac's day to be a dozen watermills are still silhouetted against the river's powerful stream. Our destination was the picture-postcard village of Saché, eight kilometres from Azay-le-Rideau. A brightly painted steel mobile made by the famous American sculptor, Alexander Calder (who had made his home in Saché for many years), slowly turned in the tiny *place*, making an amazing contrast with the ancient timbered, lopsided restaurant, the Auberge du xii siècle, opposite, and the medieval mass of Saché's château (home of the Balzac Museum).

Two months earlier, in a spring journey of investigation, I lost my way, thus discovering this delightful corner of the Loire. I had profited from the happy accident in two ways; inquiry made of three old Gauloise-smoking villagers who loitered in the square revealed that there was a local wine, going under the name of Azay-le-Rideau, and that in their unanimous, considered opinion, the finest exponent of the wine in question was a certain M. Gaston Pavy. This *vigneron* inhabited a tiny cottage across the Indre, easily accessible by a metal frameworked bridge; absolute identification would be furnished by sighting a large midden close to the cottage door.

M. Pavy was not at home: he was out, tending to his osiers, willow plantations that provide canes for the local cane and wicker-work industry – mostly carried out by posses of itinerant gypsies – but Mme Pavy was friendly enough, once she had recovered from the shock of meeting a complete stranger, a foreigner to boot. She even allowed me to taste the wine, an extremely pleasant white wine, made in dry and *demi-sec* versions, from the Chenin Blanc, or Pineau de la Loire – the ubiquitous grape variety of Anjou and Touraine. Furthermore, this sensible woman had let me purchase twenty or so cases.

The second bonus of that springtime loss of way had been a simple picnic I had garnered in Saché's only *épicerie*. I had spotted the most attractive meadow imaginable, just before I had crossed the bridge. Here, the Indre was wider, making a gentle curve around the flower-filled field. My basic fare of *baguette*, *tête de veau*, big flavoursome tomatoes and goats' cheese, *crottin*, was as satisfying as could be, taken by the meandering river among drifts of snakeshead fritillaries; the bottle of Azay-le-Rideau *sec* that Mme Pavy had generously pressed upon me only added to the perfection of the moment.

By the fag-end of July, the countryside had changed considerably; snakeshead fritillaries had long since withered away. We made our way with ungainly difficulty down what had *not* seemed to be a steep bank in early May. As we struggled through waist-high grass, Ray and Reggie had already begun to complain. I laid out the rugs by the water's edge, while the women began to butter the bread. As I uncorked a bottle of fresh and fruity Chinon, a realization of the full horror of the situation flashed into my head. Vague recollections of stories of Ray's aversion to any picnic, other than one laid out upon a damask-covered table within thirty yards of his kitchen door (preferably with candelabra *and* attendant servants) suddenly flooded back. Much worse, he was of medium stature and *very* slightly round while Reggie was a big man – in every physical sense of the word: it was horrifyingly apparent that they were *not* prepared to sit upon the ground . . .

I happened to lift my head in this difficult moment of crisis, and unexpectedly glimpsed a small whitewashed house further upstream, beyond the trees . . . the Pavy residence, of course! Talking fast and sufficiently plausibly, I succeeded in cajoling an ill-humoured Ray into accompanying me on a quick visit to one of my most recent suppliers; reluctantly, he allowed himself to be gently pushed back up the slope towards the car.

This time M. Pavy *was* at home, and very friendly too; he seemed remarkably undisconcerted at the sudden appearance of two Englishmen. Courtesies exchanged, and the house's wine re-examined, I attempted to explain my guests' predicament, but lacked the French for 'stool'. When elaborate dumb-show had ultimately conveyed my companions' plight, Gaston simply picked up two of the family's best dining chairs and stowed them in the car. In fact, it was difficult to dissuade him from donating the entire set of six. Then, gilding a fine gesture, he insisted on presenting us with three bottles of his excellent wine as accompaniment to our meal. '*Bon appétit*', he bellowed, as we drove away.

Ray fared well enough – though he *did* look rather odd, sitting on a formal dining chair in the dense, tall grass at the Indre's edge. His large friend was not so fortunate; having selected a dampish spot on which to place his seat, sheer weight and uneven posture contrived to sink the chair's back legs into the soft soil: Reggie performed a spectacular backward somersault – avoiding a chilly dip in the river by a whisker and, thank goodness, *not* damaging the piece of furniture in the process. The Pavys had gone out when I went to return the chairs, so I left them concealed behind the dunghill, with a roughly scribbled note of inadequate thanks.

The following day Liz and Esmé returned to England, leaving me to chauffeur the two men around the Loire. Things seemed to go from bad to worse. After a 10 a.m. pause at a brasserie in Chinon to imbibe a couple of restorative Pelforth *bières brunes* apiece, we crossed the Vienne, admired the fine views of Chinon's fortress château across the water, and proceeded towards a luncheon engagement with my good friends, Claude and Hélène Ammeux, at Saint Nicolas-de-Bourgueil.

As we passed through the stone-built village of Candes Saint Martin, with its fortified Romanesque church, I remembered how impressed I had been a year or two before when I had made the short walk up a gentle incline behind the church, to see a magnificent panorama of the confluence of Vienne and Loire. Reggie and Ray reluctantly agreed. I soon wished that they had not. The gently sloping three hundred yards of my flawed memory turned out to be nearly a kilometre of muddy one-in-five assault course. When I had finally got them to the top, Ray resolutely refused to turn to view the panorama, gazing inland in sulky silence; Reggie spoke – though in unflattering and uncivil terms.

When we had slithered back to our vehicle, and my silent passengers had clambered aboard, I reflected that we were on our way to visit one of the best cooks to be found among my circle of grower friends: Hélène's tasty food would be certain to mollify my angry companions. As we passed between the gate piers of Clos de la Contrie, my heart sank: the apparatus for a barbecue had been arranged upon the lawn. There would be no succulent morsels of fresh fish doused in a subtle, complex sauce, no casseroled pheasant, no roast goose or kid on this occasion, none of Hélène's delightful concoctions; simply blood-red lumps of tough, inedible beef.

Such was the case, the meal practically a disaster, compounded when a cheerful Claude adjusted his new hi-fi equipment to maximum volume behind Ray's deckchair, blasting the silent man with strident popular music. Instead of our habitual aperitif of a good *méthode champenoise* Vouvray from just along the Loire, some wretched salesman had perpetrated a sale of a disgusting *cuve close* creation that rejoiced in the name of 'Café de Paris' – the vinous equivalent of a perfume favoured by those female friends of my youth who could not run to 'California Poppy', making do with 'Evening in Paris' instead. Ray winced as he took a first tentative sip of this travesty of a beverage, and did not return to his glass.

The red wine saved the day: Claude's Clos de la Contrie is a light, yet complex wine. Typical of all good examples of Bourgueil and Saint Nicolas-de-Bourgueil, the wine ages remarkably well, developing exquisitely delicate aromas that truly call to mind the allusions to violets and other hedgerow flowers that are so irritating in the literature. The light flavour is frequently no less fascinating, exhibiting an elegance and a vibrancy that can be utterly entrancing, with undertones of truffle tastes and a faint nutty, earthy spiciness. Venerable were the bottles with which Claude honoured these important visitors, and marvellous were the soft, beauteous liquids that the cellar-stained bottles dispensed. A peaceful serenity crept into Ray's face as he savoured the splendours of the Ammeux antique vintages; as the warm summer's afternoon wore on, we *all* relaxed as the vintages gradually went further back in time.

That I had not fully alienated my friend became evident a few months later, but the kindness of his action in turn created its own sequence of problems. It was agreed that Yapp Brothers should provide a special offer in association with the *Observer Colour Magazine*. We conferred and tasted and made our selection; Ray wrote an emotive description of the wonders of my wares and, in due course, a rather stolid full-page colour photograph of the chosen bottles appeared in the paper.

Any elation at such glorious publicity was annihilated by the news on the same day of my brother's unexpected death in Paris. While I was in Paris, making the necessary arrangements, orders for the *Observer* selection began to arrive in volume.

It was difficult to take much interest in trying to deal with the avalanche of orders but, at the same time, it proved to be a helpful distraction in that it helped to ease the immediate pain. One thing became clear: my former mythical secretary now needed a real live successor, so I advertised for help. A number of charming young ladies applied for the position, but no thought was required in making my selection: Felicity Maw-Forbes obviously had to be followed by Miss Cerise Lawson-Tancred – I could hardly believe it to be true.

Cerise, it must be confessed, was a fairly lousy secretary, being far more interested in matters equine and canine. While her Great Dane puppy devoured every shred of upholstery in her Mini, Cerise did her utmost to cope with the complexities of typewriters and the arcane mysteries of dictation. She did her level best to get me through the problems created by the highly successful *Observer* offer but, before too long, we mutually agreed to part company, while still on reasonably good terms. Cerise did *not* emigrate to

Australia and eventually achieved success in the world of estate agency. The next girl was a competent typist and held the fort for ages.

Beer to Milk to Wine

Hinckes Mill House was quite unsuitable for general office purposes; the main hallway must have presented a curious sight to casual callers – with office equipment jostling with normal domestic furniture and various artefacts; privacy was practically impossible. At the same time, the strain on storage capacity (with noticeably increased sales following Cyril Ray's propaganda) was fast becoming intolerable; the garage was by now packed to the ceiling, all the non-clinical space at my surgery held a generous quota of cases of wine, and unmade-up stacks of brand new cartons occupied a doctor colleague's garage loft.

My printer, a long-term friend, had recently moved his business from premises just along the High Street from my surgery to some spacious Victorian warehouses down by Gillingham's railway station, and very near the river Stour. A semi-underground cellar with its own independent entrance was superfluous to his needs. Christopher generously put this dank basement at my disposal, asking for no reimbursement, save for a *sotto voce* suggestion that an occasional bottle might, in falling from my hands, *not* break on the cellar floor, but make its way to him.

Gillingham and district had suffered more or less serious flooding over many years in approximately seven-year cycles, but no one had ever bothered to tell me this. It began to rain . . . and rain . . . and rain. As the flood waters mounted, I struggled to get home by every possible route. As the police put out 'road closed' signs, one last choice of route seemed to hold out a favourable chance – until I reached a flood pouring past Gutch Pool Bridge.

The level lapping the bridge parapets seemed to indicate a not impossible depth of water, but the flood *did* extend at least a hundred yards along the road. Citroën cars are ingenious, with a sophisticated system of hydraulic suspension that permits raising the chassis. Setting the appropriate lever to give maximum height above the tarmac, I drove slowly but purposefully into the rapidly rising flood.

A third of the way across, water started to seep beneath the doorsills; at the halfway mark, on the bridge itself, the engine gave up the ghost. Luckily, the vehicle was a heavy machine – otherwise I would soon have been sailing down the Stour to Gillingham and the sea. It was when the muddy water swirled above my knees that I had to face the grisly realization that I would have to abandon my brand new, two-days-owned Citroën CX Familiale with only 140 miles on a mileometer that was now in imminent danger of being submerged. When I had uncomfortably waded up the long farm track that led to the nearest human habitation, I was glad that I had waited sufficiently long for the local anaesthetic to take maximum effect the previous week, when I had extracted an aching molar from the man who opened the door. My entry into Mere, towed by the farmer's tractor, was *not* a happy one. I felt even more foolish (but immensely grateful) when the insurance company's inspector wrote the soggy, smelly vehicle off.

My gloom became despair when I viewed the Gillingham cellar on the following day. Oil-polluted water reached two-thirds up the walls; pallets of cartons had collasped, the sodden cardboard having disintegrated; a flotilla of bottle labels floated on the scum. Most of Christopher's employees were also dental patients, so willingly lent a hand. The scars created by that disastrous deluge have just about been healed by time. The strain of paying daily or even more frequent visits to the station-side basement, collecting cartons from my medical friend's loft and lugging ever greater numbers of heavy cases of wine through the surgery to my awaiting car had already become arduous and very boring; the ghastly incident of the flood confirmed a nagging thought that it was high time to look for premises with sufficient capacity to house me *and* my wine.

After a few false trails, the milk factory in the middle of Mere became my target. I had been offered the rambling premises a year before by their then owner, Unigate, at which time the half-acre complex of buildings had been in immaculate condition. At that time I neither had access to adequate funds nor could justify such a massive investment for such a modest business. In the interim, a firm of London property dealers had acquired the place, with a view to future development. When the local planning authorities had been reluctant to grant planning permission for the Londoners' grandiose schemes, the owners had practically put out notices encouraging vandalism. Presumably they thought that, given time, the site would be completely cleared by happy scavengers, so that they then might have their way. The scene was one of devastation, the whole place one colossal mess – *and* the asking price had increased dramatically. However, nothing else in the area was remotely suitable for my purposes so, taking a deep breath, I bought a dilapidated milk factory.

I lay awake at nights, deeply worried about the finances of the whole foolhardy venture and desperately wondering how to make the place usable and inhabitable. The core of the complex, a bewildering array of brick buildings, had been rendered a hideous eyesore at the hands of eager, voracious marauders; the pantiled roofs were no longer there, metal light conduiting had been blow-torched away for the value of its copper, and fixtures and fittings were no more. The small amount of open space was obstructed by the carcasses of giant boilers; the whole establishment was, literally, a nightmare.

In the end, the solution was absurdly simple. I sold the boilers for a pathetically inadequate sum, but at least the lucky purchasers removed their massive bargains promptly (six months later an irate scrap-metal merchant demanded to know where his boilers were – he had commandeered the property as a temporary and totally unauthorized scrap-yard: I blandly denied all knowledge of the matter).

The decrepit central buildings, with their widely varying floor levels, simply had to go. A bulldozer drove around in ever-increasing circles, flattening everything in its inexorable path. One section of unwanted wall had to be left standing for several weeks: a pair of pied wagtails had built their nest in a crevice, and were sitting on their eggs. Almost daily I see wagtails bobbing round the courtyard, presumably descendants of that original pair. Instead of proving a headache, the mountainous heaps of rubble neatly filled out the unevennesses of floor level, so nothing had to be carted away. Only when the bulldozer was in danger of razing the peripheral warehouses to join the massed piles of masonry did I ask its driver to desist from further destruction.

Only a sixty-foot industrial chimney was spared from annihilation, and now decorates the courtyard in splendid, free-standing isolation: a monument to the past. A courtyard *had* been created, a handsome and extremely serviceable open space that was entered by a large double-doored gatehouse (needing only a portcullis to complete a resemblance to a castle entrance). The stone cottages that make an enormous L-shape to the right of the gateway are the oldest part of all. When interior walls were removed to create larger domestic spaces, I felt guilty at the destruction of ancient craftsmanship: beneath wallpaper and nineteenth-century plaster, horizontal strips of elm were filled in with mud and horsehair – a method of construction of several centuries before.

The last of what appeared to have been four or five cottages contained a curious relic that remains a mystery. Clearly as old as any of the other former dwellings, a room of twenty feet by fifteen, it has only half a floor. The far side of the room consists of a sunken pool, bounded on three sides by an external wall; the four feet of water contained in the astonishing basin being absolutely crystal clear. An indiscernible spring wells into the pool from below, any excess water trickling away through a small hole at one end – no matter how much water is extracted, the original level is rapidly regained. Immediately christened the 'Grotto', this strange phenomenon has been gradually refurbished over the years. The rough floor has been tiled and two ceramic murals adorn the wall – Dionysus, and a young ancient Greek woman bearing a cup of wine. A conservatory built on to the garden wall is reached by a small humpbacked wooden bridge that spans the pool; a lead mask of a water god spouts an endless stream of water into the basin beneath (courtesy of a recirculating pump concealed beneath the bridge) where several dozen bright-hued Koi carp slowly meander through the translucent pool.

Seventy years ago, when the milk factory was in its heyday, churns of milk would be lowered into the constantly cool waters of the tank during the heat of day, before being taken the five miles to Gillingham station by horse and dray, to be loaded aboard the evening train to London.

Several warehouses form the eastern flank of the property, the white-tiled walls of one indicating its former dairy status. The circle is completed by what used to be stabling for the milk factory's carthorses, with a hayloft up above – a building that figures in the foreground of a turn of the century photograph depicting the topping-out ceremony on the completion of the chimney. The edifice is encased in ramshackle-looking wooden scaffolding right up to its sixty-foot summit; bowler-hatted workmen stand solemnly on every level. The stables have provided ideal offices since the premises were purchased in 1973.

Local history relates that two brothers called Lander, who lived in the cottages in the early nineteenth century, started up a small brewery to assuage the town's thirst – presumably drawing their water supply from the basin in the 'Grotto'. Business fell off badly when the temperance movement arrived in Wiltshire; rather than risk total bankruptcy the Lander brothers, with commendable presence of mind, attended a public meeting at the nearby Temperance Hall, where they duly signed the pledge, and then briskly handed out business cards stating that the brewery would reopen as a cheese and bacon business several days later. If medical or governmental authorities should ever enforce punitive or repressive legislation against the sale of alcohol, I very much hope that I would be able to display a similar adroit ability to change course with such flair and enterprise.

The principal decorative feature of the courtyard is a large fountain that represents a distinctly worrying *folie de grandeur*. Within two months of taking up residence at what had rapidly been renamed the Old Brewery (as being far more consonant a title for the premises of a wine merchant than 'Milk Factory'), I woke up one morning with an irrepressible desire to commission a stone fountain of the type that adds such charm to the pretty villages of the Southern Rhône. I sent off photographs of half a dozen different Provençal fountains and well-heads to a well-known London firm of monumental masons. A week or so later, an impressive blueprint arrived, depicting the most attractive fountain that one could hope to see. The quotation for the cost of making the artefact was staggeringly high – £1,000 in 1973 – but the thing was so incredibly handsome that there was nothing else for it but weakly to confirm acceptance, in the hope that the problem of finance would sort itself out in the course of time.

A few months later a lorry drew into the yard, loaded with enormous lumps of masonry – the constituent pieces of the fountain. No warning had been given of impending delivery; it was 6.30 p.m. on a November night, raining heavily, the lorry driver was a young man without assistant, an always unreliable second-hand fork-lift

truck was temporarily out of action, and I was on my own. In the end
we succeeded in rolling each immensely heavy block down a couple of
stout planks. The cockney delivery lad was quite concerned at the
size of the pieces of stone that had become detached from the parent
chunks in our heroic struggle to discharge his precious load. I did my
best to convey an air of carefree nonchalance as I made some
amusing quip about us having added valuable antiquity to the object
in the course of removing it from the truck.

Any niggling worries regarding the knotty question as to whether
or not my latest and already jumpy bank manager might possibly be
a secret admirer of fine examples of the mason's art vanished when
the fountain was finally assembled: it was truly wonderful.

When I turned a corner by the Mule du Pape (where the *balotte*
players engage in hotly contested, day-long matches) on my next
journey through the Rhône, I was so highly disconcerted that I very
nearly drove through the thing; there, in the middle of Châteauneuf-
du-Pape's diminutive square stood *my* fountain! The extreme depth
of my regrettable lack of acquaintanceship with the villages of the
region that I had elected myself to represent was manifested by a very
basic misapprehension. I had imagined that the fountain at the Old
Brewery was a compilation of architectural elements selected from
the half-dozen examples of the genre shown in the photographs that I
sent to its manufacturers in London – for that was exactly what I had
suggested that they do. I had completely failed to register that the
beautifully drawn side elevation had shown an accurate represen-
tation of *one* fountain alone: that of Châteauneuf-du-Pape itself.

Not *quite* a facsimile; despite the heavy instant ageing and antique
distressing inflicted on delivery, my version was still in rather better
condition than its parent, and also somewhat larger. Once I had
recovered from the shock, I was really very delighted that I had
accidentally acquired the fountain of Châteauneuf-du-Pape (if I had
been a wealthy American, I suppose that it might have made life
easier just to buy the original).

It appeared that the bank manager was as much a barbarian as his
predecessors and was *not*, unfortunately, a devotee of fountains, or of
wine, but I repaid the debt . . . eventually. That bizarre investment
turned out to have been the best thing that I could possibly have
done; the courtyard was made immeasurably more attractive by its

exotic addition, and has enhanced the premises greatly ever since. Each spring is heralded by the placing of terracotta pots of massed agapanthus against the fountain's edge; the dismal advent of full autumn signals the time for their return to the conservatory. The Châteauneuf fountain was the Old Brewery's first embellishment; Auguste Clape's splendid antique hydraulic wine press, the mighty Plissonier travelling distillery from the Haute Savoie and all the other wine tools and artefacts that decorate the yard, office and 'Grotto' gradually made their way to the Old Brewery over the succeeding years.

In March 1973, just before the Old Brewery began to figure in my life, I saw an ideal way in which to make a couple of well-merited 'thank yous'. My birthday is on St Patrick's Day – 17 March; I suddenly discovered that Edmund Penning-Rowsell and Cyril Ray celebrated their birthdays on the day before. The Café Royal had recently bought some wine from me – by courtesy of Ray, who enjoyed a special relationship with the Trusthouse Forte organization (and, indeed, with Lord Forte himself). Over the years, the company had availed itself of much generously volunteered wine consultancy assistance from Ray and, as a useful gesture of gratitude, had arranged that he should have special concessionary rates whenever he chose to lunch or dine at its celebrated Regent Street establishment – something that he did quite regularly at that time.

After an agreeable luncheon together in the Grill Room (a gloriously and flamboyantly rococo room that is almost over-exuberantly ornamented with fine-figured caryatids, and plumply pouting cherubs up to all kinds of mischief – all so heavily gilded that the whole experience is rather akin to that of dining inside some particularly grandiose fairground organ), Ray introduced two important directors of the Trusthouse Forte empire – which helpful encounter subsequently led to my being allowed to hold a press tasting in their cellars below Regent Street. The cellar master of the extensive vaulted wine stores at the time was a sprightly, witty cockney, who was very much a 'live wire' – and something of a 'wheeler-dealer' on the side. When I got to know John better, I found him to be both amiable and helpful. Having realized the coincidence of the three birthdays, and that 1973 marked Ray's sixty-fifth birthday (and Edmund's sixtieth), I immediately sought the cellar master's assistance in setting up a special celebration.

The advice and co-operation of Carlo, the Grill Room's marvellous *maître d'hotel*, was also an essential; together, we worked out a seemingly straightforward but, in its way, impressive menu. The particular help that I required of the cellar master was in finding a wine that would mark Ray's year of birth, *but* still be accessible in price. John did his level best to accommodate me, but it was a commission that was far from easy. Finally, we were in luck: it was simply his hard luck that Ray could not be counted in the vanguard of devotees of port – the only wine to be found among the Café Royal's extensive stocks of venerable bottles that bore the necessary date, the magic 1908, was a solitary bottle of Cockburn port.

Summoned up from cellar to table in the normal way, for the appraisal and pleasure of some Croesus of a tycoon, the going rate would have been a huge sum – far more than I could possibly have afforded, even if I had enjoyed the favourable opinion of the most complaisant bank manager in the world. John was just as disappointed as I was that the feast would not be able to terminate with such a grand and appropriate flourish: both he and Carlo were particularly fond of Ray. He worked hard to adjust the price of that tantalizing bottle downwards, towards my severely circumscribed horizons, but the gap remained impossibly immense.

Then an idea struck me, and I put it to the eager-to-be-helpful man: what effect would my handing over a bottle of Château Latour 1934 from my ex-Leeds treasure trove, for addition to his archival stocks, have upon the matter? A miraculous one, it turned out. The Café Royal boasted an extraordinary run of vintages of Latour, a collection of which the restaurant was inordinately proud. The one vintage that was needed to complete the remarkable succession just happened to be that of . . . 1934! John would be delighted to make a straight swop; the Café Royal would add an example of Château Latour 1934 to its collection, while my birthday luncheon party would end on the dizzy high note of Cockburn's 1908.

I think that the affair passed off rather well. With our wives, we made a convivial sextet. The first course (something good, but simple – new season's asparagus, I think) was partnered by a Loire white wine from my list, Marc Brincard's elegant La Roche aux Moines

1969 from the fascinating *appellation* of Savennières. The red wine was near perfection, a delicious Châteauneuf-du-Pape, Chante Cigale 1964 – a wine that Noël Sabon had guarded in large oak *tonneaux* for at least eight years, a fast-disappearing traditional treatment that had subtly muted the wine's powerful richness with complex undertones. It was just as well that the wine had stature: the main dish was rather, well . . . ostentatious. A huge silver-domed trolley was wheeled to our centrally positioned table by a posse of reverent waiters. Carlo himself was attending to our needs; he it was who threw back the carriage's covering – to reveal its occupant: a whole spring lamb roasted to succulent, pink perfection.

I was contentedly working my way through the slices of mouth-melting meat when Carlo gently plucked at my sleeve. Another person in the Grill Room was insisting that he too should share our lamb. Carlo had pointed out that the poor animal had been privately commissioned, but the supplicant continued to utter his plaintive demand; ultimately he had entreated the *maître d'hôtel* to consult me on the matter. Naturally, I signalled my assent: Egon Ronay had gone up in my esteem; he was patently a man of excellent taste, discernment . . . and persistence.

We chose from the usual full selection of puddings, but there was one wine only to accompany them: a lovely Bonnezeaux, a sweet wine from the Loire, Mme Fourlinnie's vibrant, yet dulcet, Château des Gauliers 1947. I had decided that we would leave the cheeses until the end of the feast – in deference to the port. The Cockburn's 1908 was very, very good; a little attenuated by the passage of time, perhaps, but still extremely viable, and a splendid finale.

I have to confess that I was slightly saddened when ten years afterwards, in the course of a conversation with Ray, the subject turned to his experiences of antique port. He told me all about the marvels of a stupendous specimen from the early years of the century (his birth year, 1908, to be precise) that he had once been fortunate enough to share – Cockburn, he seemed to remember. He had the clearest recollection of the wine . . . but had completely forgotten the occasion.

Foire aux Vins d'Orange

My most exciting present of the season arrived on 4 January 1974, in the form of a letter from a M. Vincent Alessandrini, *commissaire général* of the *foire aux vins d'Orange*. M. Alessandrini had written to ask me to participate as a judge at the most important of all Rhône wine fairs; my joy at receiving such a signal honour was unbounded! I promptly cancelled all engagements so that I would duly be in attendance in Orange exactly two weeks later.

Having no precedent to go by, I was not at all sure just how smartly dressed a wine fair judge should be. I solved the problem by packing all my decent clothes in a large and shabby suitcase. The voyage across the Channel was as uneventful as had by now become routine; the night ferry from Southampton to Le Havre was fairly quiet – only a dozen or so winter sports fanatics journeying to the ski slopes of Austria and France, and a handful of check-suited French juggernaut drivers playing vociferous poker in the bar.

The trees and hedges of Normandy were leafless, but the bare branches made a pretty sight, sparkling with thick white hoar-frost and hung with diamond-beaded spiders' webs, as I sped towards Rouen, and then on again to Paris. Once the start-stop-start congestion of Paris had been safely negotiated and I had picked up the A1 *autoroute* at the Porte d'Orléans, the trip went well – and fast. Contented to be so well on schedule, and very happy to be heading south once more, the notion of a small detour off the motorway occurred to me, as midday and Burgundy rapidly approached.

It was pleasant to be in Beaune again. A *demi-pression* of beer in a marketplace bar helped to restore my travel-jaded tissues. For January, the weather was exceptionally mild; the sun was shining in a cloudless blue sky. Rather than eat an indifferent, undercooked *bifteck* and chips in an overheated and overcrowded motorway service station café, why not get together a picnic, and pause to savour it beside a minor Burgundian road? Why not, indeed! The very act of buying the various ingredients is half the pleasure of a picnic in

At 7.30 p.m. precisely, and as neatly turned out as circumstances allowed, I set off for my rendezvous with charming Mme Point.

Having had only the slightest acquaintance with grand eating-houses, my apprehension was considerable as I slowly circled La Pyramide, and parked before the shrine. Though approaching eighty, Mme Point was still on duty in the hall – looking remarkably alert and energetic for her venerable years; she gave me a fleeting smile of recognition, then her eyes quickly travelled down to check that my attire was not *entirely* too disreputable. My having bought a tie since our afternoon encounter seemed to reassure the lady; graciously, she ushered me on, into the temple precinct, and placed me at a luxuriously appointed table.

In the event, I can remember remarkably little of the experience, despite its being the culmination of so many years' wishful and wistful ambition. I quickly realized that any worries about apparel had been groundless; apart from two apparently staid and very correctly dressed elderly couples, my only other fellow diners comprised the members of a pop group, scruffy young Frenchmen with dirty jeans, casual shirts open to the navel, rather a lot of chunky gold necklaces and bracelets – and not a tie between them. The cigarettes that those exotic young people passed amongst themselves smelled unusually aromatic. I began to relax, and to enjoy the special splendour of the surroundings.

It is obvious that the food I ate that January night was utterly delicious – I well remember that being the case – but the *wine* was the evening's greatest revelation. I already had a deep admiration for the gorgeous white wine of Condrieu, with its intense, complex and intriguing smell and flavour, so reminiscent of spring hedgerows, and of subtle, cloying musk; a half-bottle, even at that dizzy price, fulfilled all that I wanted and expected of it; it was the red wine of the district, the Côte Rôtie, that proved to be a knock-out (emotionally, not literally); and such a curious grower's name too, M. Robert Jasmin.

The ancient *sommelier*, a contemporary of Mme Point, seemed amused and pleased by my overt enthusiasm, and expressed the opinion that M. Jasmin might be quite amused by the sight of an inarticulate Englishman on the morrow.

M. Tomasi's directions actually worked: to the right of Ampuis' grimy *salle des fêtes*, behind the church and bang next to the level crossing, stood a more than modest house, the object of my quest. My luck was in; there was M. Jasmin, hosing out some small barrels in the yard. A large, burly fellow of slow, decided movement, Robert smiled with quiet self-assurance as I strove to stammer out my compliments for his lovely wine. No matter how small his production may be, or how unsophisticated the man, a master *vigneron* is always well aware of the virtue and the superiority of his handiwork, and accepts such tributes with easy grace.

I must have passed some sort of appraisal, because I was then invited to inspect the tiny cellar, and to try the contents of the handful of barrels that rested therein. Some mutual respect must have been engendered, because I was then ushered into the family's kitchen, hub of the household. We sat on two of four upright dining chairs; the other furnishings of the kitchen–sitting room consisted of a large television set, a huge refrigerator, an enormous antique armoire, kitchen table and a capacious, workman-like cooker.

As Robert reverentially removed the cork from a bottle that carried fifteen years of bottle age and dust, and (a rare sight in rural France) decanted its precious contents, I realized that I had achieved a minor rapport with this agreeable and gifted man.

Even so, there was to be no Jasmin Côte Rôtie forthcoming for me that year, and precious little the next – eager local demand was well able to mop up the small quantity made, and would have been delighted to cope with ten times more. Eventually, a special campaign had to be mounted to secure adequate amounts for British cellars.

For me, there is always excitement in the air as I drive south, on a *route nationale* or down the motorway, the Autoroute du Soleil, from Lyons and Vienne, towards the historic town of Orange. I enjoy a sense of happy anticipation at any time of the year – though I am there most frequently in winter, when vines and trees are dormant. In the heat of full summer, massed blooms of pastel-shaded oleanders create the most exotic division between the *autoroute*'s carriageways; *always* there are clumps of teardrop-shaped dark cypresses to show that one is entering Provence. The cottages and white-walled houses dotting the surrounding hillsides begin to have terracotta tiles upon their roofs, a form of pantile that has not changed since the Romans inhabited the region two thousand years ago. At the edges of fields, tall windbreaks of bamboo give essential protection against the full force of the mistral, the powerful, pervasive wind that can drive people to distraction.

Passing the medieval fortified village of Mornas, built completely in a giant cleft in an ochre cliff that is surmounted by a thick-walled seigneurial castle, the unmistakable conical bulk of Mont Ventoux comes into sight, over to the east. The huge extinct volcano is a natural feature that dominates the countryside for many miles around. Orange must now be near; then, on the outskirts of the town, the *route nationale* makes a tiny deviation, to swing around the original Roman entrance to the settlement – a now battered but still magnificent *arc de triomphe*.

Not that I felt particularly cheerful as I drove into Orange that Friday afternoon. The euphoria of my encounter with Robert Jasmin that morning had dissipated the further south I went. I knew that the *commissaire général*'s office had reserved me a bedroom at the town's best hotel, the Arène, in the centre of the *place*, but I had no idea what would be expected of me – or of what the programme might comprise. The old-fashioned room was comfortable enough (the vast bed could easily have slept five), but I felt extremely unsure of myself as I descended to the hall. There appeared to be no one of even vaguely official status about the place, from whom I could ask information. The letter of invitation had mentioned the hotel arrangements, but otherwise had merely specified that I should present myself at the scene of the tasting at 8.30 a.m. on the Saturday.

I seated myself beneath a vestigial palm, desultorily turning the pages of a tattered copy of *Paris-Match*, feeling particularly aimless, and hoping all the while to be rescued or to be given helpful advice. The Arène showed no signs of possessing a restaurant; I had just about given up my vigil, and was about to brave the cold outside in search of somewhere modest and inexpensive (the previous evening's *grande bouffe* at La Pyramide had proved to be even more inconceivably expensive than my wildest estimates of possible cost, and now funds were worryingly low) in which to eat a solitary supper – when I was delivered from my plight in a most unexpected way.

I was being addressed in English, *and* by a clearly recognizable pronunciation of my name! Standing over me was the slim, tall form of a smiling Peter Hallgarten, asking me whether I was ready to proceed to the evening's official banquet.

The only London wine shipper to have appreciated the merit of Rhône wines in the long period of their doldrums, when the world did not, Peter had put together by far and away the best range of good examples of Rhône to be found on any wholesale list. His selection of Châteauneuf-du-Pape (from the cellars of the Reflets – an association of individual growers particularly devoted to excellence) was especially fine: in one of my earliest lists, when I had had nineteen different Châteauneuf-du-Papes in stock, six had been culled from Peter's London cellars. I had always found the wine trade to be generous, but no one had been more so to me than the man standing beside me then. By this stage, I had managed to create my own system of sources of supply, and had ceased to buy from him – indeed, had become something of a rival – but his kindness remained utterly undiminished.

There *was* a hotel restaurant, Peter explained, as he led me through the square to its location, a hundred yards away. The room was the scene of the greatest animation: a huge, jostling congregation of all shapes and sizes of *vignerons* of the region, conversing by means of wild gesture and even wilder shouts. A glass was thrust into my hand, and I was urged to quaff its pleasant contents. The whole affair was far more reminiscent of a particularly robust, rustic harvest supper in a village hall than any official dinner.

The hubbub was quelled momentarily when the distinguished-looking, grey-haired M. Alessandrini (whose film-star good looks made him look more like an amalgam of Yves Montand and Jean-Paul Belmondo than the organizer of a provincial wine fair) managed to call the assembly to order for just long enough to be able to indicate that it was time to find a seat at table: dinner was about to be served.

I have very little recollection of that evening – save that it was joyous in the extreme. Heaven knows what we ate – but I know that it was both copious and good. Of the wine, I am more certain; it was an ocean of young white Châteauneuf-du-Pape – in the earliest stages of the party, at least; presumably we must have gone on to red in the course of the long meal. One of them, and I strongly suspected the *blanc*, had given me a head-throbbing hangover when I slipped back into semi-consciousness next morning: the French expression for the malady, *gueule de bois* – wooden tongue – seemed peculiarly apt . . .

My mentor was awaiting me when I stumbled down the stairs at 8.15 a.m.; it was high time that we were off, to start the morning's work. The setting for the tasting was incredible, *and* unlikely. Orange is famed for the richness of its Roman heritage, antique monuments abound in every corner of the town, but the Théâtre Antique is, I think, unique in Europe – if not the world – both in its size and in its state of glorious completeness. Other pedestrians were hurrying in the same direction, through narrow streets, towards the amphitheatre, but their (and our) destination was *not* the vast stone-benched arena, where fine performances of full-blooded Italian operas are played to two thousand rapt listeners on balmy nights in summer; rather like ants scurrying into a narrow crevice in the soil, these serious citizens were popping into a doorway hewn from the solid rock to the *side* of the enormous edifice, into a narrow passageway leading below the banks of seats.

Although I did not know, that was the last year in which the *foire aux vins* was held in the galleries and catacombs that honeycomb the hill below the *théâtre*. As a location it was fantastic: any cinema director would have been enthralled to happen upon such an emotive *mise en scène*. Trestle tables had been set up in every passage and cavern of the complex – each bearing its quota of unidentifiable bottles. Flickering candles illuminated the Dantesque scene. I was escorted to my particular table, and introduced myself to the five men already there: three Frenchmen (two growers, and a *négociant*), a Belgian shipper and a Swiss wholesale wine merchant (both countries whose historic interest in the Rhône has until recently far exceeded that of Britain or America). Not too bad a group, I thought, as I furtively swallowed an aspirin that a secretary at the entrance desk had donated upon request.

I am ashamed to reveal that my efficacy on the team was sadly limited; not only did I feel a complete and utter novice, but for the first few samples I had the greatest difficulty in concealing the degree to which my hand was shaking – such had been the excesses of the previous night. In point of fact, my dereliction did not matter in the least. My co-judges turned out to be an opinionated bunch. The wines under scrutiny were two-year-old Côtes du Rhône Villages and most of the twenty before us were tolerably good. The Frenchmen were completely chauvinistic (naturally), and showed the strongest inclination to award gold medals to the lot; the Belgian and the Swiss were good wine-men, clearly accurate tasters, and were not prepared to be railroaded into such a ludicrous stance. I saw my role as an upholder of the peace, and an averter of out-and-out fisticuffs.

Ultimately, and with *my* casting vote, the rest of Europe enjoyed a modest but satisfying victory over local France: one competitor was assigned a gold medal, the silver remained unbestowed, and two lucky *vignerons* were to be honoured with a bronze apiece. As we put down our tasting glasses for the final time, any temporary animosity was immediately put aside with hearty handshakes; then we went in different directions, to assay other tables' wines.

I was delighted to run into one or two growers with whom I had done business in the past, and to meet one or two other Anglo-Saxons, with whom I rapidly made friends. Gradually we filed out of the grottoes into the wintry sunshine – the celebratory luncheon was being held in a school two streets away. The numerous throng (several hundred of us had been incarcerated beneath the *théâtre* for the best part of five hours) strolled round to the luncheon venue, chattering happily as we went.

By now, I was becoming accustomed to the immense scale of French mass public catering, so was not quite as astonished as I would otherwise have been to see the school gymnasium laid up for four or five hundred guests (wives and families were allowed to join in the festivities, now that work was done). My new-found friends and I quickly found an unobtrusive corner where we could sit together, and survey the proceedings from a safe vantage point. The first bottle was being passed around, when I felt a tap upon my shoulder. I turned to find Peter Hallgarten once more by my side.

When I suggested that he should join us, he acquiesced, but went on to explain that, as the most distinguished British Rhône specialist present, my name was on a card at a place on the *table d'honneur*: he would happily replace me in the corner, while I must transfer myself to the top table. I rejoiced in the compliment, but detested the idea; I drained my glass and reluctantly made my way through a packed hall to the appointed place.

The situation was *far* from promising. My neighbour to the left was a large Italian woman, whose husband imported Rhône wine into Italy: she spoke no French or English, so our exchanges were limited to gestures and smiles; on my right I had a very correct individual, the *général* of a military air base to the east of Orange; I did not imagine that we were going to find a great deal of common ground – we did not. Feeling cheated that Miss France (a stunningly pretty girl, but who currently had an unfortunate facial rash) had been placed an unbridgeable five seats away, I decided to make the best of things by paying attention to the undoubtedly superior wine with which the table had been blessed.

As I happen to have my copy of the menu, I can relate that the banquet went like this:

Pâté croute

Jambon

Rosette

Bouchée à la reine

Noix de veau

Petits pois à la française

Plateau de fromages

Corbeille de fruits

Tarte maison

Café

Quite a modest line-up – compared with some such banquets that I had by then endured.

As I started to toy with my *bouchée à la reine*, I glimpsed something unusual from the corner of my eye: an electrician was tinkering with a microphone just behind M. Alessandrini's chair. A wave of nausea went through my body, as a hideous realization crept over me: it would, naturally, be obligatory for the president of each national delegation to make some form of speech at the banquet's end . . . *in French*. In the light of how I then felt, I can wholeheartedly substantiate stories of flesh going hot and cold. I am surprised that I did not faint – it must have been a close-run thing. Certainly, *that* was the end of the meal for me, so far as eating was concerned. I pushed away the puff pastry and cream-cooked chicken and spurned every dish that followed, as I desperately racked my brains to come up with a solution.

A first thought was to sidle from the hall and telephone home with terse instructions so that, half an hour later, some functionary of the fair would search me out, to break it to me (in a subdued whisper) that my entire family had been killed in an automobile accident . . . but, somehow, that did not seem to be a viable way of escape. The golden fillet of veal put before me was of not the least interest, so I occupied myself with a fairly imposing Châteauneuf-du-Pape instead. My motherly Italian neighbour became worried at my abrupt loss of appetite – but, of course, I was unable to explain.

It bore upon me that I would simply have to make the speech – I, who had hardly opened my mouth in public in my native language, before a score of people – I was going to have to totter to the microphone, and say something intelligible to five hundred attentive faces . . . *in French*! I decided to go easy on the wine. I can also vouch for another phenomenon said to occur under difficult circumstances: my visits to the *toilettes* were far more frequent than anyone else in the concourse; of that I am quite sure.

Preserved for possible posterity on the back of the menu for the *déjeuner* of the *foire aux vins d'Orange*'s *présentation des echantillons* of 19 January 1974, is my putative discourse for the day. (Actually, looking at it now, I am pleasantly surprised at the distinct *Frenchness* of my feeble effort – although I suppose *that* reaction stems from a worrying lack of progress since.) The front of the card bears the Paris address of a new acquaintance – a fellow, as it happens – not that of spotty but still delectable Miss France.

Time stood still (yet another truism that I am prepared to vouch for); well . . . went exceedingly slowly, before the ghastly banquet drew towards its grisly end – *Macbeth* had nothing on it.

As might well have been supposed, the French dignitaries were thrilled to have access to a high-powered public address system. Vincent Alessandrini, by virtue of his office, was allowed the first half-hour upon the infernal thing.

Not prone to making much effort in the translation of French public speeches, my attention level had ebbed even lower than usual on that particular day. Monsieur le préfet de Vaucluse rose next, for a voluble harangue at the assembled multitude. The other French politicians curtailed their speeches, somewhat prudently I thought, in the light of audience discontent. Then the national delegations stormed upon the scene. An unfortunate truth is that Britain seems to be the only country in Europe that has difficulty with French; obviously the groups of wholesale shippers had nominated their very best Francophones as spokesmen, but it was eminently dispiriting to listen to their poised and fluent orations. Rhône wine, I realized, would henceforth be barred from Britain; when I had done my worst, the British might do well to avoid the Rhône for quite a few years to come. The Belgian (my erstwhile colleague) was succeeded by a German, by a Swiss (not of my jury), by a Dutchman – even the Italian woman's husband made a short and surprisingly comprehensible speech.

Time had run out; every other country had had its say. My eyes began to blur, as the master of ceremonies announced that, on behalf of the *délégation britannique*, the speaker would be . . . M. Peter Hallgarten! I cannot remember what he said, but it was admirably short, and to the point – some sort of admonishment to the *vignerons* of the Southern Rhône that they should not be avaricious, and should endeavour to keep the price rises to the barest minimum – excellent stuff like that. Secretly, I was rather pleased to realize that Peter's command of French was not all *that* vastly superior to my own, and his accent not much less atrocious either.

When I buttonholed him later, Peter admitted that he had taken a slightly mischievous pleasure in leaving me in ignorance of the need for speeches, and in failing to notify me of the one that he had prepared on the train on his way down through France the day before. As I made a last-ditch effort to catch up on lost drinking time, I magnanimously forgave him.

A vineyard tour by coach for the foreign delegations on the Sunday morning, followed by a luncheon at Mère Germaine's in Château-neuf-du-Pape, was the only official obligation that remained on the agenda, so Peter and I decided to dine together. Currency restrictions were in force at the time, so he was little better off than I; we agreed that somewhere small and unpretentious (and above all cheap) should be our goal. Luckily, we fell upon a tiny restaurant in an alley opposite the Théâtre Antique: appetizing aromas of good cooking were wafting through the door as we entered the Bec Fin, invitingly warm, with red check tablecloths.

A fortunate choice, we realized, as we surreptitiously eyed our fellow diners: several elderly citizens who obviously ate there daily – their serviettes were kept in a set of wooden pigeon holes – and two Belgian wine shippers, the shorter, stouter and balder of whom was my colleague of the morning. He waved us over when he had spotted us, and the two men insisted that we join their table. Of course, we were happy so to do. A most agreeable meal ensued. The dishes were all simple home-kitchen sort of food: pickled herrings with raw onion rings and a mound of potato salad that only a French waxy type of *pomme de terre* can give; rich, flavoursome terrine of hare; moist, pink, succulent *foie de veau* with *pommes vapeur*; tender, tasty casseroled pork chops – the sort of food that my mother might have cooked – if she had been French and cared for cooking!

The wines were equally simple, but honest, made from grapes and satisfyingly cheap – so we drank rather a lot, as we cheerfully and noisily swapped wine trade stories in a weird mixture of French and English. Coffees and *digestifs* finished, the Belgians called for the bill. They would brook no argument when we tried to pay our share. If we were so fortunate as to meet up again in similar circumstances (perhaps at next year's fair?), they would allow us to play the hosts. With warm handshakes and '*à demain*', we emerged back into the alley.

As we passed a small cinema, I noticed that the last performance was just about to start. With the money we had earmarked for dinner still in our pockets, I stifled Peter's protests and dragged him into the auditorium (remembering to give the usherette a tip). Later, I felt that honour had been satisfied, and that I had taken sweet revenge: the film was a particularly gloomy piece by Ingmar Bergman – with an English soundtrack or subtitles, it would have been extremely heavy-going; in Swedish, and with French subtitles, it was utterly appalling. I felt that inflicting unintelligible intellectualism on my poor compatriot gave him as miserable an experience as had been my purgatory at lunchtime. We ambled back to the Arène, the best of friends once more.

Gastronomic Warfare

Rhône wines were at last beginning to be appreciated in Britain; I was gratified to find that at long last sales of the best single-vineyard wines, particularly those of the Northern Rhône, were going well. It was time to lay siege to the all-important growers who produced the finest wines, so as to secure a sensible proportion of their product for an awakening British wine-loving public.

Robert Jasmin was target number one.

Two years after our first (for me memorable) meeting, I had managed to build our allocation up to a heady thirty cases. Judith and I decided that it would be sensible, and possibly pleasant, to invite the Jasmins to lunch with us at a restaurant in their district; we realized that Mme Jasmin, Josette, had a job somewhere in Ampuis, so that lunch at their kitchen table would never be a possibility.

Showing a deal of initial reticence, they were eventually persuaded to accompany us to an unpretentious but pleasant restaurant on the other side of the Rhône. When we finally found Domaine de Clairefontaine, on the plain beyond the river, I, as host, urged our guests to take the *menu gastronomique*, selected appropriate wines, and generally tried to be handsomely expansive. The meal, I noted regretfully, was, frankly, not much good. One of the red wines was in poor condition, so I was forced to sort the matter out with a less-than-helpful *patronne*.

The first inkling that, perhaps, my grasp of the situation might be less than perfect came when a bottle of champagne joined us at the table, in partnership with the puddings – and a most excellent (and costly) *marque* it turned out to be. Josette, who has impeccable taste in such matters, had left the restaurant fifteen minutes earlier on a nose-powdering pretext, paid the bill and organized this festive wine.

We made an even more concerted effort to play host the following year, but again failed miserably. When I pleaded bladder weakness, in order to quit the one-star Magnard's dining room (in Vienne) and settle the account, Josette recognized the tactics and caught me in the act. She it was who paid.

Then we hit upon a solution; we arranged to stay at the Hôtel Bellevue at Les Roches-de-Condrieu for several nights, and the Jasmins were invited to dine. The *patron*, old, taciturn, gloomy, monosyllabic M. Buron, a former rugby star, was threatened with non-payment for our entire stay, if he allowed the Jasmins within a hundred yards of the dinner bill. Victory at last!

As may be imagined, these skirmishes had led to a warm friendship and, thank goodness, rather more of the precious production began to filter our way.

Eventually we were successful in inveigling Robert and Josette into spending a few days in England. We hit them with everything we could think of: Indian food, spicy Szechuan dishes, stolid English traditional and many excursions, until, *en route* to the airport, we went to the Waterside Inn at Bray for a farewell celebration. Robert was thrilled to see his beloved Chevalière d'Ampuis in a key position on the opulent Roux wine list (the magnitude of the asking price, marked up threefold, escaped him).

An excellent and convivial meal together, then a pair of exhausted Jasmins were pushed aboard a plane: I suspect that they started to plot their revenge on that flight back to Lyons.

I think that I was lucky to come home alive from my next trip to the Rhône; it took weeks for my liver to return to anything like normal. Robert and Josette had conspired that I should arrive in Ampuis to coincide with the annual wine fair. This is a two-day affair that takes place in the *salle des fêtes*, an extremely basic village hall, where the growers of the district offer their young wines to all-comers for a few centimes a glass.

The entire area turned out for the occasion, with what seemed like all Vienne and a good half of Lyons. A dense mass of overcoated humanity bore me forcibly around the trestle stands; the glass in permanently upheld arm was constantly refilled – no charge for honoured guests!

Being the most celebrated of the dozen or so growers in the commune, Robert's table attracted the biggest crowd. Stuck in the middle of the throng, he beamed at one and all as he attacked the cork in bottle after bottle. The hours passed, darkness fell; towards 8 p.m.

the crowds began to disperse, and the Jasmins packed up their stand, with a mere handful of admirers savouring the last sample that they had managed to wring from the final bottle.

With the *langoustine* of lunchtime still very much in my mind (and, by the feel of it, my stomach too), food was the last thing that interested me, and surely Josette must have been exhausted after her six-hour stint at the fair? Presumably she was, but it did not preclude a sixty-mile drive into the Beaujolais for a copious meal at a friend's restaurant.

Next day, Monday, was the serious day; wines were proffered for the appraisal of trade purchasers, serious-looking men clad in heavy overcoats against the bitter cold. It was early, 8.30 a.m.; there was a perceptible coming to attention among those *vignerons* who had already laid out their tables, as a small group pushed in through the swing doors: the tiny old lady enveloped in mink was Mme Point, the old man Louis Tomasi (my informant about Jasmin, and *sommelier* at La Pyramide since time immemorial), and the elegant young man was the chef, Guy Thivin.

Well aware of Robert's respect for Mme Point's judgement on wine, I was fascinated to follow at the periphery of her undoubted aura; very serious tasting, great concentration, then a quick, apposite comment to the grower (once or twice rather acerbic – no doubt like the wine just sampled). Occasionally the trio halted for a whispered conference before proceeding to the next man's wares. I was relieved when the party wound up with Robert, and realized that the circuit had been planned to this end.

Although Mme Point had made at least a token annual purchase from Robert and his father before him for what seemed like always, the relationship was no sinecure: that I could deduce by the tiniest glimpse of anxiety in Robert's eye as he proffered a glass of his Côte Rôtie.

All conversation ceased as the old lady warmed the glass between her hands, then lowered her head for an exploratory sniff, and then another; a thoughtful sip, a prolonged rolling of wine around the mouth, a quick, expert expectoration, and Mme Point proceeded to analyse the wine with what to me, barely able to comprehend the half of her rapid words, seemed a great deal of acumen. An aside to Tomasi, who made a note in his pocket book, and the *grande dame* was gracious enough to indicate what quantity of the current vintage should be laid to rest in the corner of the Jasmin cellar for the next two years, for eventual transfer to her own famed *cave*.

A few pleasantries for the journalists, a practised pose for the photographers, then Mme Point shook hands with Robert, with the Mayor, practically shook hands with me, and led her small contingent out into the cold January morning, leaving in her wake a visibly relieved M. Jasmin and one highly fascinated English bystander who had prudently made sure of his allocation the day before.

Soon after this the real business of the day began. I was quietly greeted by a functionary of the association of local *vignerons* who introduced me to my fellow judges: a veritable galaxy of well-known oenologists and viticultural politicians (well known in France but confusing to me).

My anxiety was quite unnecessary; I was there as an honour, a compliment to Robert, a token foreigner, the first ever to be asked to participate in the ceremony of selecting the finest Côte Rôtie of the previous vintage. Any opinions that I ventured to voice went totally unheeded; were not, I think, heard; I can take no credit whatsoever for the fact that when the names of the medal winners were announced at the end of an interminably long and, as far as I could tell, extraordinarily boring speech made by the *consul général* that afternoon, Jasmin was awarded the gold medal and another grower friend, Emile Champet, the silver.

The official luncheon at the unpretentious (not to say downright rough) restaurant across the street was a relaxed, low-key affair; all very jolly, as I squeezed in among the growers, who looked distinctly uncomfortable in their Sunday suits, but a matter of luck as to whose wine one fetched up against. An opportunity to taste everyone's soon came; as the ties came off, and the temperature rose, bottles were passed from hand to hand. A noisy, animated debate as to the virtues of this wine, the demerits of that, was interrupted only by the arrival of huge bowls of *pâté de foie de volaille*, *gratin dauphinois*, cardoons and rich tasty venison.

Later, after the long, long speeches, when even M. Gérin, mayor of Ampuis, had run out of steam, the medals were awarded. A flushed but jubilant Robert happily accepted the congratulatory handshakes of neighbours and colleagues, and the whole thing was taken as a very good reason for another, longer look at the prize Côte Rôtie. Josette had anticipated this reaction and had a battery of bottles at the ready.

Somehow I had failed to observe the enthusiasm my fellow judges had been showing for the Jasmin offering during lunch. Robert had responded to this mark of attention by inviting a small, select group to make the descent to his cellar, when the official proceedings should be over. So, several *sommeliers* from celebrated restaurants (two were female, and pretty) and a couple of oenologists straggled from the hall, over the level crossing and down into the tiny cellar. The place always seems remarkably crammed by very few barrels so it was a fair feat to get us all in.

The selection of *invitées* had been faultless: practised and opinionated debaters all. Each sample drawn from each *pièce* by long glass pipette inspired a leisurely though prolonged analysis and intricately detailed discussion. It was, in fact, all highly informative: I learned a great deal of the mysteries of the *vigneron*'s art over the next two hours.

Eventually Robert wanted to demonstrate an older wine from the wood; his eyes alighted on two tiny *pièces* in a corner, with the chalk-marked legend 'Mme Point' on each butt-end. Quite excellent, we concurred, but it crossed my mind that the four similar barrels marked 'Yapp' might as likely have been broached, had I not been present. No doubt they came into play on the next such occasion.

Then, of course, on to bottles, retreating back in time. Once or twice customers arrived to give Robert momentary distraction from the business in hand, and once Josette dashed in to get replenishments for the stand back at the fair, where there was apparently still plenty of hectic action.

At long last, even the French were reduced to silence by the sheer splendour and wonder of the 1947 wine that Robert had unearthed from a dark and cobwebbed recess. With perfect timing, Georges, Robert's venerable father, appeared to accept with grace and courtesy our fervent expressions of admiration for his creation, with the quiet air of knowing it to be perfectly justified homage.

It was after 7 p.m. before the party broke up, Robert very happy (as well he might be) and only slightly tipsy. The two of us snatched a quick snack in the kitchen, *saucisson*, bread and walnuts, before going to investigate what might have befallen poor Josette. Luckily, her elation served to mask exhaustion; she was exchanging banter with a few remaining, distinctly unsober bystanders.

We packed up the stand, the fair over for another year; then an ever-ebullient Robert proposed that we drive to Lyons for a celebratory dinner at a particularly favoured restaurant, and this we did. I was in a state of near-collapse from exhaustion (and the wine consumed, too, I suppose); at the very last, even the indefatigable Jasmins showed signs of flagging.

The next two days continued at much the same dizzy pace; tasty little repasts fifty kilometres in one direction, seventy in another: I would not have credited anyone with planning a gastronomic revenge with such thoroughness and care.

Finally, when my liver was giving every symptom of irretrievable collapse, Josette announced the venue of my farewell dinner: the *coup de grâce* was to be inflicted in Vienne, *chez* Point.

A glass or two of remarkably drinkable champagne (a commodity rather thin on the ground in the homes of your average French grower) in the kitchen, and off to Vienne for our rendezvous with Mme Point. We were received most graciously by *la patronne*; I became aware that this was an occasion of more significance than I had guessed.

Robert Jasmin had been the star supplier of wine to La Pyramide for years, as had his father before him – this I well knew; what I had not realized, though, was that this was the first time that the Jasmins had been there for fifteen years. Mme Point was hugely delighted at their presence and her warm welcome encompassed me too. Champagne arrived at our table, compliments of the house; we leaned back in our chairs to await the best that M. Thivin and his team could furnish us with.

Then I was presented with an exceedingly difficult chore. It must be remembered that these, my generous friends, were somewhat limited in their experience of wines beyond their deep personal knowledge of their own and neighbouring *crus*. Robert handed me the encylopaedic wine list, and politely asked the waiting M. Tomasi to heed my every word. This would have been a tough assignment under normal conditions; knowing that I would not be allowed anywhere near the paydesk made the task awesome (particularly at those prices). In the end, I succeeded in making an excellent compromise between quality and cost; the solution consisted of a very decent Sancerre, modestly priced away from its own region; then the most amazing Beaujolais, a venerable bottle of Moulin à Vent 1942 (so Louis Tomasi said: the label had been long lost) a deep, full, delicious wine that emanated enormous distinction, and a giveaway at seventy francs.

Finally, a perplexing but beautiful Loire wine that should have been crisply dry but, due to the mysterious transmutation that time can work upon the Chenin Blanc, this Coulée de Serrant 1949 had become a rich, luscious, haunting dessert wine, near black in hue; a wonderful experience, and that for a mere one hundred francs.

And the food; a trio of first courses to titillate our plates: *mousseline de grives* with an elegant salad (I find that the guilt induced by munching thrush, no matter how delicious the dish may be, is a sure preliminary to retributional heartburn), delicate sweetbreads encased in light, airy pastry, a *mousseline* of trout, with a wondrous sauce; even after enduring the Jasmin plot to kill me by gastronomy I could appreciate the sheer finesse of this cuisine. I languidly pushed some *turbot en champagne* around the handsome plate: delicious.

A welcome diversion occurred when Tomasi brought M. Thivin to pay his respects to Robert but, rather too quickly for my stomach's liking, he hurried back to his *domaine* to organize our *carré d'agneau*. At some point between courses we took delivery of a tasty and refreshing *sorbet de marc de Viognier* which is supposed to let all that has gone before slip down a little to create more space. Perhaps the room was needed for the fierce little goats' cheeses on tiny sticks. These *barats* are the highly specialized product of one single goatherd, and are to be obtained, if your name has been on the waiting list since birth, from one stall in the vast market hall of Lyons. I prefer to forget the puddings; I am positive that they were magnificent: the waiter wanted us to try them all.

Having deposited a vulgarly huge bouquet on Josette's lap at her place of work the following morning, I fled to the airport. The flight had been cancelled; had the Jasmins not yet given up? I took care not to return *chez* Jasmin, and walked the streets of Lyons until it was time to take the evening flight, mercifully not cancelled. When I limped into the house, I commenced the rigorous alcohol-free diet which was to last for nearly two months; little by little I began to formulate plans for the welcome with which we would greet Robert and Josette upon their next visit to Britain.

The gold medal diploma hangs in our office: Robert thought that it would make a good souvenir of my first appearance as a judge at the *foire aux vins* of Ampuis.

Such was the sort of self-sacrifice that was required to obtain an annual allowance of one hundred cases of Robert Jasmin's fabulous (when mature) Chevalière d'Ampuis Côte Rôtie. Not, it might be supposed, a great amount of wine for, quite probably, irreparable liver damage – but, at a little over a quarter of his annual production, a veritable fortune for those of us who truly care about Robert's marvellous wine.

Chez Chave

There was another *vigneron* in the Northern Rhône of even greater significance than Robert Jasmin. Gérard Chave was (and remains) the most influential grower of the region and, in my opinion at least, the whole Rhône Valley. I freely admit that it required no great feat of intellect or any deep research to discover that Chave's was the finest example of the greatest Rhône red wine of all, Hermitage, or to discern that Gérard was the most respected and highly applauded wine-maker to be found within the *appellation*. After all, he was the current custodian of a vineyard that had been handed on from Chave father to Chave son since 1481 – an astonishing succession of ownership that is without parallel in the Rhône and, quite possibly, in all France.

The huge, saddle-shaped mass of the hill of Hermitage must constitute some of the most valuable agricultural land in the world – scarcely less precious than the platinum vineyard plots of Burgundy, or the highly esteemed estates of the Médoc itself.

Gérard's fifteenth-century ancestor must have been a canny, prudent sort of fellow: the various scattered parcels of Chave vineyard that dot the steep slopes of the hill include a substantial strip of land that runs from the high summit to the plain below at the very point where the curve of the hillside gives maximum exposure to the beneficent rays of the sun. There, on the south-west-facing slope, Gérard has the venerable vines, gnarled and sturdy plants of the ancient, classical Syrah variety that donate the amazing depth and spectrum of nuance to his celebrated wine.

It was in that particular sector that I found Gérard and his team of *vendangeurs* upon my first visit to Hermitage at vintage time. Thus, early on in my relationship with Gérard, I was to gain a vivid insight into what it is that makes the Chave Hermitage so very special. I could immediately appreciate the severe difficulties presented by the terrain; on such a vertiginous escarpment it is difficult enough to retain a foothold, let alone pick grapes! With typical ingenuity,

Gérard had considerably eased the workload for his personnel by devising a simple sledge system; the grape-filled barrels, *bennes* in local parlance, are lowered to the horizontal on a sort of toboggan, pulled up and down the dizzy incline by the power of a petrol lawnmower engine.

At the bottom, manpower takes over; two men engage stout long poles under projecting wooden lugs set on the sides of each *benne*, shoulder the poles and march the overflowing barrel in sedan-chair fashion to a waiting cart.

The pickers, nearly all of whom have performed the same ritual for Gérard, and his father before him, over many years, moved slowly among the vines, leaving behind them what looked, to my untutored eyes, like beautiful, well-formed and perfectly ripened bunches of grapes. When I asked him about this mystery, Gérard laughed: one of the advantages of employing his well-practised team is that each member has an innate sense of what constitutes the Chave definition of the perfect grape. Those bunches, which might have well pleased Gérard's neighbours, were to be left for the small boys of Tain l'Hermitage, birds, or *possibly* the neighbours.

Thus it is that Gérard makes excellent wine in what are generally regarded as indifferent years, the only problem being that, after such a rigorous selection process, the off-vintage produces an embarrassingly small volume of delicious wine that faithfully reflects the Chave style. Only twice has a vintage been totally rejected, and Gérard will muse reflectively on the fact that the two small barrels which he kept for subsequent assessment proved to be remarkably good at the end of the day, an episode to be stored in his memory as a minor miscalculation, and a factor to be considered in the future.

The day of my visit was intended to see the finish of the vintage; an hour's work in the afternoon would have sufficed to complete the *récolte* for another year. Just as our thoughts were turning towards a well-earned lunch, an innocent-seeming cloud distributed what, by English standards, was a particularly light shower of rain. Without a word being spoken, the dozen or so men and women doffed jackets and cardigans and quickly covered the grape-filled barrels: they themselves might suffer a soaking, but there could be no question of a dilution of the wine. Happily, the weather promptly cleared; everyone was in the highest spirits as we and the grapes made the three-kilometre trip to the Chave home and *cave* at Mauves, on the further bank of the Rhône.

There was no chance of lunch until the morning's harvest had been gently pressed, and the resulting juice passed into one of the vast and ancient wooden fermentation barrels. Only when this important operation had been completed was there a near-palpable sensation of relaxation, of *décontraction*. In a hubbub of chatter, and a glow of something like self-congratulation, we tucked into the *charcuterie* which Gérard's wife, Monique, and old Mme Chave had prepared for us. These welcome victuals were washed down with copious draughts of equally robust, fairly rough, red wine, a beverage distinctly removed from the future nectar that was the object of the whole exercise, but probably much more to the taste of these men, and certainly more what they are accustomed to quaff when work is over.

Knowing that only an hour of picking remained, I naturally anticipated an imminent return to the vineyard. Time passed, the bottles circulated and nobody made a move. Gérard explained to me that the one short shower precluded further picking for the day, despite the cost of a full day's pay for sixty minutes' work the next day.

For someone who is virtually a legend in the world of wine, Gérard has a remarkably simple life-style. The busy *route nationale* 86 passes through the village of Mauves; in the dash and bustle of the traffic it is all too easy to miss the small tin *panneau* set at right-angles to the wall above the door, its faded legend, 'J.-L. Chave, Vigneron' being all that indicates the Chave establishment. This simple, ancient, rather nondescript house has served previous generations adequately; Gérard sees no reason for change.

There is a problem, however; Gérard and his wine are now so celebrated that a constant stream of admirers and devotees makes the pilgrimage to Mauves from all over the world, in the hope of meeting the man himself and, if at all possible, of gaining entry to the hallowed inner sanctum, the Chave cellar. Obviously, there is a physical limit to the number of such visitors it is possible to receive; a peephole high on the door houses a tiny television camera. Callers are surveyed on a small screen by the kitchen door before a decision is made as to the advisability of responding to a summons on the bell.

Luckily, I had taken the precaution of negotiating a meeting some months beforehand, so, having spotted the tiny name-plate on first search, I passed inspection and was admitted. It was just as much a matter of pilgrimage and reverence for me as for anyone else; the few encounters with Chave Hermitage that I had been fortunate enough to experience had engendered an enormous admiration. In fact, Gérard is the pleasantest, easiest person possible; it would be difficult to conceive of anyone who is less pretentious. His highly charged enthusiasm is another matter; the voltage is totally irrepressible, and highly contagious.

No sluggard on enthusiasm myself, it was to be expected that we should establish a quick rapport. An assault course through the cellars (an exhausting affair of some three hours) was followed by a delicious lunch that Monique had somehow made between bouts of wrestling with paperwork in the office. It was an extremely propitious first meeting, but an encounter that produced no visible results in the shape of a shipment, save for a few precious bottles pressed upon me by my generous host. With a severely limited production, and an eager worldwide audience importuning for a share, my disappointment was all too predictable.

More than impatiently, I took my place on the waiting list, desperately anxious for rapid promotion. Further visits deepened the friendship and, in the second year, virtue – or rather, persistence – was rewarded: Yapp Brothers took delivery of the munificent quantity of . . . ten cases of Hermitage. The following year saw an allocation of fifty, and so on. With the fabulous 1978 vintage I scooped the pool; no doubt to the chagrin of some worthy American importers, Belgians, Dutch, Germans, even some wine-loving Japanese, I had the tremendous luck of gaining an enormous *tranche* of this highly desirable product.

The Rhône has benefited from an incredible succession of splendid vintages over the last five years, but none has been finer than that of 1978. Gérard reckons it the finest achievement of his career to date, unlikely to be equalled or surpassed. Old M. Chave, old Jean-Louis, hummed and ha'd for what seemed an age before finally pronouncing the wine as utterly superb, fully on a par with – probably superior to – his own finest triumph, the astonishing wine of vintage 1929.

A good rule of thumb for aspiring wine merchants searching for good Rhône red wines is to remember that the nastier the stuff tastes when young, the better it is likely to be ten years later; at its birth, the 1978 Hermitage certainly fitted that template. I doubt if it is possible to convey the true horror of a full-fledged tasting *chez* Chave. Coming, as it frequently does, on the same day as an assessment of fifteen to twenty examples of Cornas with Auguste Clape, ten kilometres down the road, and at least an hour at Jean-Louis Grippat's house, seeing what he is up to with his Saint Joseph, the mind can only boggle, and the stomach gently heave.

Even with a ten a.m. start, Gérard has been known to keep Monique anxiously trying to preserve a lovely lunch for an hour or more than is reasonable; in my experience, no tasting has been completed in under three hours, *ever*. One begins to wonder whether one will glimpse daylight again. The kick-off is a quick working through the white wines of the last vintage, with an earnest debate as to just why *cuve* 12b would not fully ferment out like all its sisters, and a recounting of Gérard's various ruses to move the process along.

In fact, the answer was that he simply had to wait for the warmer weather of early summer to terminate the vinification and solve this particular conundrum. Twelve or thirteen *cuves* later, we ponder on the development of the whites of a year earlier, removing eight corks in the course of our research. One or two older vintages serve as quarter-time refreshment, before we move on to the heavy work, the big-time stuff: a startlingly in-depth study of the red wines.

Lined along a corridor connecting the two main *caves* are half a dozen large oval *tonneaux*, imported from Hungary; Gérard insists that the very best barrel-oak comes from Hungary or Russia. Each barrel represents a piece of Gérard's scattered holdings; the grapes from each parcel are pressed and vinified separately. A small chalked word on each barrel-end gives the, for me, vital clue as to which spot on the hillside we are examining; emotive names they are too – Les Bessades, Les Rocoules, Les Beaumes, Le Peleat, l'Hermitage. Gérard likes to discuss the nuances of each brew, how well or otherwise it typifies what we should expect from that corner, and in what magical proportion he should blend the wines to produce the best possible example of Chave Hermitage. Then we test some of the hypothetical combinations; some Les Rocoules, very dark and stuffed full of tannin, a little l'Hermitage, which seems to add a deal of perfume to the mix, Les Beaumes, which lends finesse, and so on. We refine the blend as we go; only when Gérard is fully satisfied that every potential aspect and angle has been fully explored do we pass on through the long, bottle-lined corridor to the next cellar and the next tiered row of small barrels, to begin the whole business again, with the wine that has had an additional year in wood.

This part of the session presents me with even greater problems; the wines are less brutal, less mouth-screwingly tannic, having had the benefit of an extra year in barrel, but Gérard is confident that I will remember exactly what our thoughts and comments about each specimen were a year earlier. These wines still represent the separate parts of the hill; Gérard is certain that I shall be as fascinated as he is to see how development may have varied from our original prognosis; worse, he expects me to speak intelligently on the subject.

This is my annual nightmare; it is a tightrope that I tread with care and circumspection. Somehow Gérard seems not to observe how perilously I wobble; my major fall, which surely must come, has yet to happen; my credit in his eyes lurches on, for one more year at least.

The mixing game comes almost as relief, although my rash opinions of last year are likely to be recalled in detail by Gérard, always computer-like where his precious wine is concerned. It seems a moment of deliverance when, finally, even Gérard tires of his alchemy, and we can turn our minds to older wines.

A fairly speedy sprint through the previous five or six vintages, and it is time to luxuriate among bottles of distinction, the glory of earlier years and former times. Such treasures are hidden away, in a dense mass of black spongy mycelium, peculiar to this cellar; it beats me how Gérard always knows what year it is that he is unearthing from that sinister sea of fungus.

These are precious moments, when the splendour and full magnificence of the Chave inheritance stand revealed: ambrosial wines, such as the legendary 1929 and 1935 (Gérard's birth year); comparative youngsters, such as the amazing 1961, that can stand proudly alongside the greatest wines of the world. Fully the peers of first growth clarets, these inestimable liquors age, if anything, more graciously; to participate in the privilege of savouring such wonders is not far removed from being a mystical experience. The fatigue and strain from having bent every nerve fibre into the analysis and appreciation of sixty to seventy young wines over the last few hours miraculously drops away; a sense of beatification (well, the nearest semblance of a state of grace that I am likely to be vouchsafed) creeps over: the world is not such a terrible place after all.

At last, we hobble back into unbelievable sunshine, bearing with us the choicest of our samples. We return to something like normality over Monique's *œufs brouillés aux truffes*, delicate, delicious *darne de saumon à l'oseille*, and satisfying but filling *caillettes* (curious bundles of spinach mixed with morsels of pork, a product of home *charcuterie*).

The Chaves have a bolthole for when the going gets rough, when the endless round of callers proves to be too demanding. High in the hills above the Rhône there is a most delightful farmhouse, set in a verdant *Heidi*-like meadow, with magnificent views down to the hill of Hermitage and the Rhône, far below. The farm has been in the family for as long as the vineyard, since 1481.

Gérard and Monique have created a retreat of great peace and tranquillity, as I well know, to my enormous benefit; it is here that Judith and I are billeted whenever we visit the Rhône. We have the great good fortune to have this charming place made over to us as a centre for our vineyard visiting, a haven to which we return after an exhausting tour of the growers, a refuge where we too can relax when the pace gets too hot.

The solid, comforting and comfortable furniture and pleasant pictures, most of which have descended from long-forgotten ancestors, are supplemented by the comforts of central heating (it can get exceedingly chilly at such a height, even in the spring), dishwasher and refrigerator, though thank goodness that the water emanates from a spring behind the house; it makes a most refreshing draught after all that wine.

The first time that we stayed at Lemps, Gérard and Monique joined us at dusk, bearing interesting looking parcels. A huge fire of vine roots was soon blazing in the enormous open fireplace; before we fully realized what was happening, a small but succulent *gigot d'agneau* was revolving slowly on a spit before the fire, while an equally appealing sea bass was gently grilling over embers that had been raked to one side. Sheer, blissful perfection; life does not hold enough of such moments.

Upon another occasion (our honeymoon, in point of fact), Gérard accompanied us up the breathtaking hairpin bends through the wood, and proceeded to carry half a dozen copper pots and pans into the farm. After giving us accurate instructions as to their proper deployment, and indicating the bottles of Hermitage of our birth years that he had left placed horizontally in the kitchen earlier in the week, he left us to enjoy what is likely to remain the most sensational take-away meal of our lives. The food consisted of the best that Gérard's *copain*, the gifted chef Michel Chabran, could create in his gleaming kitchens at Pont d'Isère.

A handsome, antiquated travelling distillery has visited the small square of Mauves each year for the past hundred years or more. There, under the yellowing autumnal leaves of grievously lopped plane trees, the vast, imposing apparatus holds court from mid-October until December, when it disappears as swiftly and as mysteriously as it arrived – to perform the same task at some other village in the hills of the Ardèche. Long the object of my admiration whenever I chanced to pass that way at the appropriate season, the massive *alambic* took on an enhanced allure when Gérard told me of an annual gastronomic treat that he had himself instituted twenty years before, by now a time-honoured custom.

Gérard is an enthusiastic and more than competent cook (something of a rarity among Frenchmen, whose presence in the kitchen is normally as critical consumer of whatever the industrious women have laboriously prepared for their appraisal and swift ingestion). Having revelled in his simple, delicious dishes – a gridful of oysters lowered on to the intensely hot embers of burning vines, shells spitting shrapnel around the room, the toothsome sauce of butter, herbs, garlic and a drop of wine in each half-shell; fat breasts of Barbary duck, all seasoned for the grill; thick slices of fresh salmon, cut in a fashion that is peculiarly French, bobbing pinkly in a spicy marinade; newly picked young garden vegetables softly stewing in a conical, earthenware Moroccan *tagine* – their recollection so mouth-wateringly vivid, small wonder that I became alert, and eagerly demanded what provender was associated with the ancient still.

A ham, a simple *jambon*, was the answer, but the unique charm of the dish lay in its cooking: the joint suspended, *à la ficelle*, in the alcoholic vapours inside the gleaming copper heart of the *distillerie* for as many hours as needed to bring the meat to aromatic perfection.

The moment of precise readiness pronounced, the ham has to be swaddled in heat-conserving cloths before being whisked the four hundred metres around the corner, to the *vigneron*'s cellar, where an expectant and semi-inebriated group of friends impatiently await its coming. The meal is by way of being a ceremony to celebrate the conclusion of yet another vintage. Would I like to participate on the next such occasion? Would I not!

Summer passed to autumn with no word from Gérard, an oversight of some kind, I rather feared. Upon our next meeting the explanation was given, and sad listening the story made.

As in every other year, and in due season, the *distillerie ambulante* had appeared in Mauves' square; the same gnarled *bouilleur de cru*, owner–operator of the apparatus for countless years, had charged and ignited the fire-box, turned various taps, set all in motion, so that distillation might begin. As always, villagers and peasants from outlying farms and hamlets crowded round to seek their places in the *bouilleur*'s busy schedule, fixing when to bring their barrow-loads of *marc*, the debris of skins and pips left from pressing the grapes, or bucketfuls of fermented fruit juice for transmutation into heady eaux-de-vie.

The law regarding distillation is exact and very strict: minute and accurate records of all transactions must be carefully kept in the distiller's smear-stained exercise book that serves as the official register. Apart from a residual handful of growers entitled to a modest duty-free quota, all must pay a bitterly resented tax of thirty-five francs a litre. A stricture that allows an easier policing of the distiller's activities is that nothing of the day's production may leave the vicinity of the *alambic* until the evening.

How could it have been that a throng of normally ultra-inquisitive, gossipy French peasants failed to spot the trap? An unknown van parked in the square, albeit marked *Boulangerie quelquechose*, should surely have excited comment? When had the locals previously seen a vehicle with windows so heavily tinted as to be impenetrable to the eye? As car after car departed from the *place*, boots heavy-laden with illicit, liquor-filled demijohns, the two representatives of the Fraud Squad concealed in the van passed descriptions and car details by radio to posses of gendarmes posted at both exits of the town. One after another, the unlucky 'moonshiners' were flagged down, politely invited to open up their boots, and fined on the spot a swingeing five hundred times the unpaid duty for each litre of contraband spirit.

Only at dusk did the hidden observers emerge, to arrest the *bouilleur de cru*, and to hustle the poor, protesting man to an awaiting police car and on, eventually, to a longish sojourn in prison in Valence. Even when his sentence has been served, even if he can raise funds sufficient to pay the massive fine, it is highly doubtful that the old fellow will again be permitted to practise his former trade: the authorities are less than happy about fully functionable *alambics* lying unattended around the countryside. Wholesale destruction of the machine is the probable outcome; it is unlikely that a travelling still will ever again grace the square at Mauves. When I called there in late November, a rather forlorn-looking ham was reposing in a carton in the corner of Gérard's cellar, waiting for normal cooking at the end of the year.

The travelling stills of rural viticultural France are disappearing almost as fast as they fall out of use. If the authorities do not destroy them, their owners, careless of any sense of historic worth, themselves break up the machines for the paltry value of the metal content. Which is why, when I learned of a *distillerie ambulante* lying unloved in a leaking barn in the Haute Savoie, I telephoned its proprietor, bargained with him, purchased the thing and arranged its carriage to these shores. A splendid specimen, fabricated by M. Plissonier and his team in Lyons in 1909, now stands in the yard at the Old Brewery, an awesome amalgam of cast iron, massy beams, brass taps, retorts and copper coils; as far as I know, the only such monster to reside in Britain. Who knows, perhaps the ex-distiller of the Ardèche would appreciate a few days' vacation in this country, when he might be induced to pass on his lore; perhaps I should suggest that Gérard brings a ham with him when he next visits Mere?

Gérard is something of a rarity among French growers, a wine lover who is keenly interested in all the wines that the world can offer. Below the farmhouse lies a vast cellar; distributed about its sandy floor are groups of bottles representing the other vineyard areas of France, Europe – even California – and Gérard has chosen well. A further instance of his tremendous generosity is that I am expected to feel free to research these wines, if and when so inclined.

Gérard is certainly exempt from my oft-stated criticism that while they make the finest wines in the world, the French are usually the least adept at appreciating their handiwork. Indeed, I know that he agrees with me; when we visit the celebrated Michelin three-star restaurant in Valence, Pic, where the Chave is the house wine, albeit highly expensive, we observe fifteen to twenty bottles of the last available vintage at various tables, being swallowed with an astounding lack of interest, and total lack of appreciation, by wealthy chain-smoking Parisians.

When I expostulate at this terrible example of Gallic infanticide, Gérard smiles somewhat ruefully, shrugs his shoulders, and points out that it is one of the reasons that it is relatively difficult for a Frenchman to purchase his wine; he prefers to allot us our high proportion in the knowledge that in Britain it is far more likely to be given the bottle age and appreciation that the wine so richly deserves. Even so, he cannot decline absolutely to furnish the cellars of distinguished chefs, such as Troisgros, Alain Chapel, Paul Bocuse, Mme Point and Michel Pic – all of them friends and fervent admirers.

Gérard's cosmopolitan, wide-ranging interest in wine and his pre-eminence in the field of Hermitage mean that he is the Rhône grower most in demand to participate in important comparative tastings – another demand on his valuable time, as are the numerous viticultural political meetings, *réunions*, which he is asked to attend. He obliges as much as possible, provided that such distractions do not interfere with his principal passion, making fine wine.

Nothing could make Gérard eschew the traditional methods that produce the epitome of great Hermitage but, when he sees good reason, he proves to be more innovative than his colleagues. The Jaboulets, of the important *négociant* house of Paul Jaboulet Aîné, in Tain l'Hermitage, are close friends of the Chaves; there is a constant lively exchange of ideas and advice between the two families.

Gérard was an early advocate of the idea of the *vignerons* forming a consortium to pay for the use of a helicopter to perform the five or six *traitements*, anti-fungal sprays, that are essential to the well-being of the vines. No mean feat, to persuade a dozen French farmers to unity of opinion and purpose.

During the seventeenth and eighteenth centuries Hermitage was renowned for a rich dessert wine called Vin de Paille, but none has been made for well over a hundred years. Luscious ripe white grapes of the Roussanne and Marsanne varieties are left on a bed of straw to desiccate to raisin-like proportions, so that each fruit produces a single teardrop of intensely sweet juice when pressed in December. The quantity of grapes needed to furnish a litre of Vin de Paille is prodigious. Several years ago, in spite of the enormous effort required, Gérard could not resist recreating this delicacy of the past. The results of his labours were two small *pièces* of traditional Vin de Paille lurking in a dark, dusty corner of the cellar, and very good it is: I prize my own small stock highly.

Adventures together . . . too many to enumerate. I particularly treasure the memory of Gérard's first visit to London; after a highly successful press tasting, and a tour of some dockland pubs, we dined at the Garrick Club with a few friends. It was evident that Gérard was much taken with the grandeur and beauty of the elegant morning room, visibly impressed by the wealth of paintings in the coffee room, and generally delighted by the sophisticated ambience of his surroundings. As the meal drew to a close, Julian Jeffs suggested to me, in a whispered aside, that we might move on to the Reform Club, in Pall Mall, for coffee and cognac; the others readily concurred.

As we strolled through Piccadilly Circus on that warm summer night, *en route* to the pillared magnificence of the Reform, I reflected that Gérard would take a lot of convincing that this was not in fact the normal pattern of my days, not my usual life-style; at the same time I fervently hoped that the price of my next purchase would not be elevated too much as a consequence of what he had seen.

On another occasion we were given strict instructions to descend from the farmhouse at an early hour. When we arrived at Mauves at 7 a.m., we were greeted by an enormous snuffling pig, at liberty in the courtyard. Gérard had remembered the interest Judith had shown in tales of the annual winter ritual of killing a pig for transformation into *charcuterie*; we were to participate in these awesome mysteries.

After the inevitably gruesome opening ceremony, the day was punctuated by halts for libations; the slaughtering was celebrated with white Hermitage (at 7.15 a.m., a trifle early in the day for me). At 8 a.m. work temporarily ceased for the consumption of a *vigneron*'s breakfast; a lot more wine (red and white) washed down the copious food, substantial slices of *jambon cru de l'Ardèche*, *saucisson*, pâté and all. Two hours later saw the traditional tasting of black pudding, *boudin noir*, the pig's own intestines encasing a dubious blend of herbs, orange water and barely congealed lukewarm blood. This delicacy is Gérard's particular delight, the finest moment of his day, but certainly not mine; the short lapse of time between live animal and tepid *boudin* severely afflicted me. I preferred to address my attention to the excellent Saint Joseph proffered with the titbit. And so it went on until, in the late afternoon, after a staggeringly prodigal lunch, the ex-pig was displayed as hams, terrine, *caillettes, fromage de tête, pâté de foie* and sausages. That evening I seemed to have lost my appetite, and listlessly toyed with a *caillette*, one of the brand-new batch . . .

When asked by a highly reputed women's magazine to nominate a Christmas present from me to me, I had no hesitation in choosing a wine. I asked for a bottle (better a magnum) of Gérard's 1978, but stipulated that it should have been subjected to the influence of some time machine – that the wine should carry twenty years of bottle age. With that advantage, the amelioration produced by the passage of time, I know that Chave 1978 would easily be in my personal pantheon of the three best wines that I have tasted, or am likely to taste.

Royal Return

Ten years ago, I pioneered the idea of an annual series of special wine dinners (and occasionally luncheons) at various venues around the country – a useful and highly enjoyable promotional scheme that ran for several seasons. The settings for those, sometimes sumptuous, feasts included some prestigious places – such as Hintlesham Hall (then in Robert Carrier's custodianship), Homewood Park at Hinton Charterhouse, Thornbury Castle and the Carved Angel in Dartmouth.

When the excuse of having to officiate at a Yapp dinner took us north to Hallgarth House Hotel near Darlington, I was unable to resist the urge to revisit the old haunts of childhood holidays and scenes of my brief career in catering.

Robin Hood's Bay was just as quaint and picturesque as I had remembered it – an avalanche of cottages frozen in the act of tumbling down the hill. Rain was pelting down like stair rods as we derived what little shelter we could against the wall of the Bay Hotel. I was reflecting that this was a typically bracing end-of-summer day for the north-east coast, when a large roof tile detached itself from its fellows and very nearly brained Judith and me. Through the curtain of water, it was just about possible to discern the grim rectangular outlines of Raven Hall Hotel, perched high upon the other headland, a mile across the bay.

When we walked soggily into the hotel's cocktail bar forty minutes later, I experienced a mild *frisson* of wickedness at daring to enter that formerly forbidden territory. Shivering, we tried to combat the seasonal chill with large measures of Laphroaig; I suddenly recalled a sweltering August night, when the pressures of a chaotic Saturday night dinner had finally unbalanced an always irritable head chef; some innocently intended remark of mine had been totally misconstrued by the heavily sweating captain of the kitchen: a razor-sharp and formidably long Sabatier knife flew from his hand in *my* direction – with full intent to kill. Fortunately (in my opinion) he missed – but only just. For the rest of that evening's service, it was deemed prudent that I should avoid the kitchen area, so my colleagues had fetched me my necessary dishes, while I skulked in the relative safety of the dining room.

Later still, in Scarborough, the heavens continued to throw down torrents of rain. It was far too wet to be able to make a tour of the pubs that used to calm my post-dinner nerves with soothing draughts of Strongarm and barley wine. We made a dash from the car into the portals of the Royal Hotel. It turned out to be the last day of the hotel's summer season; less than half the tables were occupied, so we were ushered to what had always been, in my days there, a highly coveted window table, with a view down to the harbour. A Royal Hotel waiter can *always* reckon class, I thought to myself, as I took the wine list from his hand.

Sadly, the list was a vestige of its former self, but was able to furnish us with a bottle of Bollinger and a delicious Château Gruaud Larose 1971. The elderly diners at tables around us looked positively scandalized at the reckless profligacy of my ordering *two* bottles of wine. They could not imagine the importance of the long-delayed pilgrimage.

None of my fellow waiters seemed to have survived the passage of time; all pensioned off during the intervening quarter of a century. There was no one that I recognized, though the lugubrious Yorkshireman who took our order was a classic example of the type of men I had known. The gloominess of his features implied that we would be lucky to get any food at all, let alone that it might be appetizingly edible.

Delightedly I pointed out to Judith the amazing collection of paintings by the celebrated Ruszkowski that still adorned the restaurant's walls. Tom Laughton had sold the Royal a decade or so before – presumably lack of wall space in his cottage in Scalby had precluded him retaining his beloved Polish masterpieces.

At sometime in my history (1975, to be precise), that most respectable of London gentlemen's clubs, the Garrick, had somehow been induced to absorb me into its delightful arms. In fact, I had not scrupled to take advantage of Julian Jeffs's high moral sense: when he had kindly offered to support me for election to membership of the architecturally elegant Reform Club I had politely declined the honour. Knowing that Julian was also an equally enthusiastic member of the Garrick, I had managed to convey to him that I would be far from averse to nomination for membership to *that* distinguished club. With typical generosity, Julian promptly proposed me for election to the Garrick: it can only have been his strenuous efforts (and, perhaps, the fact that the Garrick had been one of my earliest institutional customers – so that the members of the wine committee vaguely knew my name) that finally won the day. Scraping home with what must surely have been the barest acceptable minimum of supporters (but fortunately, no one knew enough about me, or my possible demerits, to put a 'black ball' in the box on the all-important day), I found myself, to my considerable surprise, a member of the august establishment – a club which I have found to be a most agreeable and convivial society.

A few years afterwards, I was browsing through the membership list when I was startled to see that my erstwhile employer, Tom Laughton, had just been elected to the club; it amused me vastly that I should be the senior member – though only by three years. Events seldom turn out *exactly* as one would wish, and my ambition was never achieved: my earnest wish that I might run into Laughton in, say, the bar or the morning room, introduce myself as his former lowly employee, and stand the old boy a glass of champagne (which I would have made sure was my own beloved Jacquesson – *not* Krug) never came to pass. Not so many years after the publication of his delightful autobiography, *Pavilions by the Sea*, Tom Laughton died peacefully, at his home in the village of Scalby – on the road that leads from Scarborough to Ravenscar, and Robin Hood's Bay.

I am happy to report that the wine list at the Royal Hotel shows signs of distinct improvement: the current managing director has just written . . . to ask me for a copy of my list.

Two-thirds of the way through the seven weeks that it took to scribble down this purging of my past, Judith and I held a small dinner party to celebrate New Year's Eve. An inspiration overtook me: the occasion would provide a wonderful opportunity to take a nostalgic look at those wines that had particularly punctuated my vinous adolescence *and* of which examples remained in the cellar – hitherto undrunk! A sextet of friends, three couples, duly arrived – not suspecting what I had planned. In the event, I was able to muster a surprisingly broad selection, the constituents of which added up to a roll-call of some of my strongest wine memories.

It had proved to be impossible to track down a bottle of Krug Private Cuvée 1949 – probably just as well, considering the price that I might have had to pay! As Jacquesson champagne had been my undisputed preference for nearly twenty years (so much so that I had insisted on making myself its British agent eight years earlier), the *vin d'honneur* for the remarkable celebration was not difficult to choose. Our guests were greeted with the assistance of a magnum of Jacquesson's gorgeously creamy *blanc de blancs*. Having not long before received a severe rap on the knuckles from Bollinger, for committing the *lèse-majesté* of infringing what turned out to be their registered trade name, 'Récemment Dégorgé' (in my opinion, a quite unreasonable appropriation of what is, after all, the description of a process), the next bottle out was of Jacquesson's marvellously elegant Dégorgement Tardif 1969 – a wine that is as good as champagne can get. (It had taken two bottles of this fine, de luxe wine to help us come up with the 'DT' riposte to Bollinger's 'RD'.)

In the context of the other wines, the Meursault was, frankly, something of a disappointment. Still a drinkable and *interesting* wine, the full-bodied Chardonnay flavour that I could recall its having had in plenty, twenty years before, had quietly slipped away.

New Year's Eve 1986

WINES

Champagne
Jacquesson: Blanc de Blancs
Jacquesson: Dégorgement Tardif 1969

White
Meursault les Charmes 1957

Madeira
Sercial 1871

Royal Return

Red
Château Latour 1934
Château Margaux 1945
Château Lafite 1953
Château Cheval Blanc 1953
Château Figeac 1955
Château Lascombes 1961
Château Mouton Rothschild 1961

Sweet white
Château Climens 1955

Port
Taylor's 20 Years Old Tawny

DINNER

Pissaladière

Smoked salmon

Roast sirloin of beef
Roast potatoes
Carrots
Brussels sprouts
Yorkshire pudding

Cheddar
Stilton

Apple tart

Judith had purposely kept the menu simple and straightforward, so as not to eclipse the wines. A mad-keen fisherman customer (a retired dentist, as it happened) had called at the Old Brewery to purchase a case or two of wine (and to swap the odd fishing story – about the one or two that had *not* got away) a few days earlier; as luck would have it, this God-sent angler happened to have had two sides of freshly smoked, personally caught Avon salmon on the passenger seat of his car. He was happy to swap the fish for wine. Simple (and delicious) it may be, but the richness of smoked salmon presents problems of perfect partnership that most wines cannot hope to match. Sercial 1871 (a vintage wine, *not* the product of a Solera dating from that year) proved to have been a happy choice – in fact, the salmon had a job to assert *itself* against the pungent nuttiness and sheer vibrant splendour of the old Madeira.

With seven red wines to accompany the roast sirloin of well-hung beef *and* the Cheddar and Stilton cheese, it seemed only fair to take a democratic vote as to what might be an ideal batting order. Oldest first was the considered opinion of the committee. The Château Latour was, in its way, the most astonishing of them all, the greatest success of the night. A staggeringly opulent bouquet presaged a complexity of undreamt-of amplitude; what might have been expected to be a potentially tired old wine was as fine as one could ever hope for. Furthermore, it improved still further over several hours in the decanter; the little that remained next morning was still radiating magnificence!

Despite some misgivings on my part, the Margaux finally lived up to its reputation; the seemingly immutable tannic hardness of twenty years before had finally softened out, and the wine truly proved its point; all legends as to its possible longevity seemed quite true. The wine's ambrosial aroma was far more richly scented than it had ever been before; its fine-nuanced flavour became more satisfying with every passing hour. On that night's showing, Château Margaux 1945 can be counted as one of the great wines of the century.

The 1953 wines, it should be confessed, suffered somewhat in comparison with their companions. The Cheval Blanc had a fine delicacy that would have enchanted us, if we had viewed it on its own – in this assembly, a now faintly fading old lady was overshadowed by her peers. The 1953 Lafite displayed an even more reticent ethereal refinement; slight, but lovely, its evanescent charms were distinctly overridden by the robustness of the other wines.

The only wine that I had had to buy in was the Château Figeac 1955; I ran a bottle to earth at that splendid treasure house of old vintages, La Vigneronne, in Old Brompton Road. Mike and Liz Berry had several bottles of Figeac 1955 in stock; the wine had been bottled in Belgium by H. Grafe-LeCocq et Fils, but seemed none the worse for that. Still in excellent condition, its savour augmented in the glasses as the meal leisurely progressed; I was relieved to realize that the wine's old ability to turn my stomach had completely disappeared.

Having managed to keep my hands off the 1961 clarets with such remarkable self-discipline for so many years, I approached the Lascombes and the Mouton Rothschild with particular interest. Both had been worth the wait. I had always carried high expectations of the senior wine; they were amply fulfilled. The Mouton Rothschild exuded as marvellously intense a fragrance as I have ever inhaled: country cottage gardensful of summer flowers lingered in that delicious smell; the rich, luscious flavour held out the likelihood of decades more of further subtle amelioration. The surprise was that the Lascombes was not that far removed from its supposedly superior neighbour in terms of excellence and stature. Its life expectancy seemed likely to be somewhat less . . . but, by now, debate was dying down, and a pleasant glow of satiated content had settled in.

The Château Climens turned out to be a minor marvel – perfect partner to Judith's delicious apple tart; the wine could have stood for pudding on its own. Now dark amber in hue, its complex honeyed sweetness was ravishingly attractive. For once, one bottle of Barsac barely sufficed for the eight of us. If there had been another in the cellar, I would have sped off to collect it there and then.

The Taylor's Tawny was as it always is, its charming but deceptive lightness carrying subtle gradations of delectable flavour. Anything more grand might well have strained our hard-worked livers beyond redemption (we agreed that *no* Frenchman could have ever stayed the course) and would have over-gilded the lily; as it was, the Twenty Years Old Tawny gently brought us back to earth.

The new year had arrived somewhere around the Mouton Rothschild stage: a most auspicious start to *any* year. An attempt at playing snooker in the small hours of New Year's Day was *not* one of the highest-scoring games in family annals (other than points amassed as a result of default and grievous inaccuracy), but clear heads later in the day were a tribute to the nobility of those transcendental wines.

Now the hunt is on, to come up with adequate justification for an annual repeat performance. Identical repetition of the event would now be rather difficult – some of the bottles consumed that joyful night, vital phials of evidence that represented special moments in my apprenticeship in the glory that wine can be, were unique examples: I have no more . . . but I am heartily glad that I was there, to assist in their imbibing.

Index